CHRISTIANITY
AN END TO MAGIC

by the same author

FOR ALL MEN

NEW THEOLOGY FOR PLAIN CHRISTIANS

CHRISTIANITY
AN END TO
MAGIC

John Baptist Walker

Dimension Books · Denville, New Jersey

Darton, Longman & Todd Limited
85 Gloucester Road, London SW7 4SU
Dimension Books
Denville, New Jersey

ISBN 0 232 51183 7

CONTENTS

INTRODUCTION

WHAT DO we really want from Christianity? Magic – or the gospel? Religion – or revolution?

It will be my contention in this book that we too often prefer the magic of religion to the revolutionary message preached by Jesus. We instinctively seek the security of a salvation that can be won by ritual performance rather than by a personal commitment to the well-being of our neighbour. We look for an escape out of the disturbing realities of our day-to-day existence rather than an increased involvement in this world, and thus try to reduce Christianity to the level of those other world-religions that have a strong thread of the magical woven into their very fabric.

This temptation is particularly apparent, as any catechist must know, in children from the ages of, say, seven or eight to eleven or twelve, when they will tend to look upon the Christian faith as revealing a secret way of winning automatically the favour of God, and will readily treat the sacraments as magical rites, prayers as spells and emblems as lucky charms. The tragedy is that a goodly proportion will never outgrow this attitude.

Indeed, I think we will find, on reading this book, that we have, in many areas of our lives, failed to do so completely ourselves. We hanker so often after the comfort and cosiness of a religion that will take us right out of this world, when what Jesus offers is a gospel that commits us to changing it. He faces us with the threat of insecurity that goes with his challenge. But he also holds out to us the certain hope that the kingdom he is calling us to help him create is already among us and will finally be fully established in glory.

Christianity is, in this sense, an *anti*-religion. It opposes radically those escapist elements to be found in most other faiths. If we are to be true to its directives, we must consequently be on our guard against the attractions of magic, and seek to rid the outlook and behaviour both of ourselves and of the Church from any attachment to what men generally regard as religion.

THE REVIVAL OF MAGIC

A RENEWED INTEREST in all things magical seems to have arisen in the west today, particularly among the young. Indeed, the fact that topics like astrology, witchcraft or occultism are no longer the preserve of a few eccentrics is reflected in the way those sections of the entertainment industry that cater more for young people have been quick to respond. One thinks, for example, of Polanski's film *Rosemary's Baby*, with its black magic theme, of the picture magazine *Man, Myth and Magic* that was sold so widely in this country a few years ago, or of the popularity of songs like *Aquarius*, from the musical *Hair*, with its assertion that the planets were ushering an era of love and peace.

There seems to be, at the same time, a revival among the young of an interest in religions. This is not to say (as any clergyman will readily agree) that young people are at last flocking into the churches, nor (as any teacher of religion will regretfully testify) that they are especially keen to learn about the more traditional forms of Christianity. It has been the fashion, in fact, among certain small but nevertheless influential sections of the young to turn rather towards the religions of the east – to Zen Buddhism, perhaps, or to Hinduism, with its practices of yoga, krishnaconsciousness or transcendental meditation.

Nevertheless, a new kind of concern seems to be spreading from California (so often, whether we like it or not, the centre of cultural movements among the young, and the image, much enlarged, of the way western society is going) about the person of Jesus of Nazareth. Fundamentalist forms of Christianity, seen in such groups as the *Jesus Freaks* or the *Children of God*, apparently thrive on the west coast of America, and bid fair to make Jesus, not drugs, the way of life for many a former flower-child.

The creed of these groups is simple. It is that of extreme evangelical protestantism, and based upon a literal and uncritical acceptance of the Bible as sole and adequate source of all truth, and upon a certain kind of religious experience as the assurance that one is saved. This, the basic message of the 'old time religion' of the U.S. Bible belt, has been adapted, however, so as to chime in more agreeably with the style and meet more directly the emotional needs of many young Americans. And, again, we can gauge the strength of this new trend by taking note of the growing number of gospel-style songs that appear in the pop music charts, or by the Broadway success of the musicals *Superstar* and *Godspell*, where Jesus, it appears, is being promoted as the new cult hero of the young.

It is interesting to see, too, how, as so often with such movements nowadays, the tendency is towards some form of communal living. The drug culture brought about its own kind of commune. A distaste for middle-class standards of family life has produced phenomena like the street people. The attraction of the magical draws hippies to Glastonbury or to Katmandu. Young people – whether from within or without the institutional Church – are trying to experiment with new forms of community living that are specifically Christian. And some have even donned the saffron robe and joined Buddhist ashrams or the Hindu Hare Krishna movement.

In every case, these varied groupings have one thing in common. They exist as an act of protest. They exist because their members have found western society in some respects so defective that they have been driven to try and create something better.

But what makes this revival of what many would call superstitious or discredited beliefs so strange is that it was all so unexpected. The advance of science and technology, so we had thought, was progressively (and rightly) desacralising nature, and taking the mystery more and more out of the mechanics of the universe. Just as we no longer had any reason to see the hand of the gods in earthquake or thunderstorm, so we had increasingly less excuse for constructing meaningful patterns in the stars or seeing the planets as controlling our lives. Even the romantic significance of the moon waned rather rapidly when our television sets revealed it as little more than a dead cinder in space.

At the same time, we were progressively (and rightly) de-mythologising Christianity, and making it more and more secular. As Christians, we were less ready to speak of a world of the spirit or of the supernatural, as though this were a realm apart from and hovering over the world that real men inhabit. Instead, we were coming to realise more intensely that an otherwise largely incomprehensible deity we call God is to be encountered above all and most surely in a Christ who is himself met with most effectively in the human community.

The sharp decline in religious practice in the west seemed, furthermore, to indicate that modern man was no longer interested in the official Christianity of the churches, or indeed in religion at all. This was apparently especially true of the young, to whom the concerns and preoccupations of the ecclesiastical organisations appeared to be irrelevant or even downright hypocritical. Indeed, some theologians seemed positively to delight in the fact that church membership was dwindling at so fast a rate. This, they contended, was a sure sign that the era of establishment was over. Western man no longer accepted Christianity automatically as part and parcel of his cultural heritage. He questioned, challenged, and in large measure discarded, the faith of his fathers.

And this was a good thing. For, depending upon their own point of view, the theologians tended to look upon the decline in two ways. For some, the Church was never meant to be a large and popular organisation, but the hidden, humble, insignificant society it had been in the days of the New Testament. For others, the Church had become so hopelessly, even arrogantly, out of touch that she both needed and deserved this humiliation. Only thus, deprived of members and of money, would the Church be forced to repent, and to rethink effectively her message and her mission.

At all events, it seemed that only the hopelessly old-fashioned would dare, in the second half of the twentieth century, to talk of the *conversion* of England or of Russia or of any other land, or of a forthcoming *spiritual revival*.

Indeed, most of us would, I suspect, doubt the value of expressing the Christian mission in such terms, heavy as they are with the overtones of nineteenth-century spiritual imperialism. But we would also doubtless agree that, as aims, they seem farther away than ever from realisation.

In such a climate, then, how are we to explain this renewed interest in magic and the religions, which, though certainly no mass movement, is nevertheless of real cultural significance in that it is especially felt by influential groups among the western young?

The causes are, it seems to me, roughly threefold.

1. The interest of some is apparently aroused by the promise of an *epiphany*, or revelation – of an experience that will convince them that the everyday world is either unreal, or at least unimportant, or else very different from what they had hitherto been led to understand.

Beginning, perhaps, with Aldous Huxley and his American experiments with mescalin, but finding its most influential prophet in Dr Timothy Leary and his preaching of the liberation to be gained by the use of marijuana and L.S.D., drugs have provided, for some, the means to this new vision of the world.

Both Huxley and Leary were interested in drugs as aids to mystical experience. And it is interesting to note how Leary, when at the height of his popularity with the American young, advocated, along with pot, Hindu ideas on the value of meditation and the chanting of the mantra, the sacred song that is said to spread the blessed influence of the heavens upon the earth.

The Beatles, significantly, followed the same path, in the sense that their songs, too, were at one time very much concerned with drugs. Then, about the period of their much-publicised retreat with the Maharishi Mahesh Yogi, they began to turn their attention, as had Leary, to the spirituality of Hinduism, returning from India to compose mantra-type songs that are basically repetitive, like *All You Need is Love*. Later, we find George Harrison recording mantras like *Hare Krishna*, and also introducing a mantra into his own very popular composition, *Sweet Lord*.

They had, it seems, been won over (like the youthful American and British converts to the Hare Krishna movement who could once be seen singing their mantras down Oxford Street, London, most days of the week) by the Hindu idea that the world as we know it is mere *maya*, or illusion, and that one of the ways to break through this deceptive veil of matter is to meditate on the ultimate spiritual reality, *Brahman*, and to imitate his manifestations in the Lords *Krishna* and *Rama*.

Astrology, too, represents the search after an epiphany, even though one suspects that the current craze on the campuses for searching the heavens to find out the future of man is intended partly as a rebuke to the middle-aged, who put their faith still in scientific discoveries that seem to have brought more harm than good to the race as a whole.

2. Witchcraft, however, is *sacramental* in its approach. It seeks after the sacred *thing*; or rather after the particular formula or spell, object and gesture that together make up the magical rite and thus give one power over the forces of nature for whatever purposes, good or ill. In distinction to religious ideas of the epiphany type, witchcraft celebrates, honours and makes use of the material world – the human body and the elements of the universe – either because it is itself sacred, or because (in Satanism) it can be employed in the service of the Evil One.

3. A similar taste for rite and ceremony is frequently to be found in groups with a more *eschatological* approach to reality – those who feel that, in one way or another, 'the end is nigh'. Indeed, one of the purposes of *Hair* seems to have been to give ritual expression to a hope that –

> When the moon is in the seventh house,
> And Jupiter aligns with Mars,
> Then peace will guide the planets,
> And love will steer the stars.

For others, however, this is the age not of Aquarius but of the flying saucer, with intelligent, superior and beneficent beings from other worlds hovering about our earth and influencing our lives to try and lead us away from final disaster and into the paths of peace.

Or again we are on the verge of that blessed time that has been prophesied in strange and cryptic ways by wise men of old, by the builders of ancient temples and trackways, the sages of Stonehenge or the seers who designed the Great Pyramid. And so one finds a concentration of hippies at midsummer eve on Glastonbury Tor, waiting for the new age to begin when they shall be able to live once more as little children in a world of wonder and delight.

Yearnings of this kind for an age of gold help to explain the present youthful interest in the Arthurian legend or the popularity of *The Lord of the Rings* and the whole imaginary world of Tolkien and the fairy tales.

The desire for some kind of saviour-hero that seems to be felt so widely among the young today may focus itself upon mythical redeemers like Arthur, Krishna or the gods; upon modern liberators like Che Guevara, Ghandi or Martin Luther King; or even upon the great religious leaders of history, the Buddha, Jesus and Mahomet.

Though rejecting, by and large, the Christ of Christian dogma, the young seem perfectly prepared to accept him as their superstar – as a man who was on their side, a drop-out from straight society, a protester against the status quo, a preacher of love and peace, a martyr for the cause of freedom. Presented as a pop idol in *Godspell*, for example, he seems to be, not so much the Word incarnate as the incarnation of the adolescent predicament.

It would be altogether too glib and superficial, however, to detect in these trends a Christianity only slightly off-key. It would be tempting simply to say that what I have labelled very loosely the revival of magic really represents a present-day quest for the Church. But it will not do.

True enough, Jesus Christ has been held by his followers from

St Paul onwards to be the full *epiphany* or revelation of God, the great *sacrament* or sign of God's presence, the final *eschaton* or goal towards which God is drawing us, and thus the real *soter* or saviour whom God has sent us to free us from our sins. The Christian, therefore, shares with a significant section of the contemporary western world an approach to reality that seems nominally very similar.

On the other hand, however, these modern tendencies betray, in many important ways, a search after *religion*, as this has been commonly understood in the history of the human race. And precisely in so far as they do (and because I believe that Jesus came to overthrow religion of this kind) I would hold them to be tendencies we must renounce as profoundly un-Christian.

I say 'renounce', and not 'ignore' or 'condemn', because I feel that the attraction of religion (as opposed to the gospel of Jesus) is so strong as to be constantly making inroads into the Church itself, which in consequence often displays an outlook all too plainly at one with these non-Christian trends, substituting weakness and capitulation to the spirit of the times for the witness and confession to which it is bound.

But what is it about this present age that urges Christian and non-Christian alike to take refuge in religion? What, in particular, leads the young to hanker after visions and magic and dreams?

Largely, I would think, a feeling of *disillusionment, insecurity* and *helplessness*.

It seems very clear that a serious disillusionment with western society is widespread among the young today, and especially among the more intelligent and vocal young. This advanced civilisation of ours, for all its boasted technology, breeds a materialism and competitiveness that almost inevitably leads to violence, oppression and the most terrible of wars. So frequently the churches as well as the politicians appear to be lending their weight to the support of this system, while education seems merely to be preparing the young to take their allotted part in the process. In other words, our computerised society turns people into objects to be manipulated by a certain group – the 'establishment' – so that it may retain and increase its own power, position and prestige. Thus, instead of helping the young come to realise with rejoicing the glory of being human, the manipulators merely train them for work that is often degrading and sterile, but which is necessary for the support of the system. And so we find young people protesting against establishment and system, and the ethic of work that keeps it going, and applauding, instead, the value of play.

Distrust of the system also helps to account for that further distrust by the young of rationality. They fear that when their instructors present them with information in patterns and forms that are claimed to be logical and reasonable, what they are really doing is indoctrinating them to accept the debased standards of a social set-up they find to be corrupt, or at least suspect.

In preference to what McLuhan would call the 'hot' media of information-processing, like print or human speech when these are made the vehicles of scientific or rational thought, many young folk would apparently rather turn to media that are more 'cool', and where, instead of being bombarded with facts and arguments, they are drawn into human events to become a part of them, experiencing and celebrating life rather than interpreting and analysing it.

The philosophies and ideologies that motivated their elders and that inspire political revolutionaries of their own age group seem capable of producing only a divided and destructive society like our own. They have apparently turned out to be such untrustworthy guides to human living that many of the young feel on surer ground if they take their evaluation of life from the novel, the theatre, the cinema, television, light shows, 'improvisations', 'happenings', sensitivity groups (in a more or less increasing order of coolness).

They reject *explanation* in favour of *celebration*. Life is a mystery that we cannot pretend to understand, save at our peril. The most we can do is experience it, accept it, become involved in it and try to improve its flavour here and now in ways of love and peace.

⋇ The young also feel insecure. They are the ones, after all, who are especially threatened by the appalling evils that hang over the future, and many of which technological man has himself created. They feel menaced by those fearful deterrents of the great powers, the nuclear and biological weapons of destruction; by the connected problems of over-population, world poverty and hunger, and the deep injustice of a southern hemisphere that grows steadily poorer largely as a result of the greed of the nations making up its northern counterpart; and by the steady poisoning and pollution of the environment through the blind acquisitiveness of men.

And yet, they feel powerless to do anything about it. Even the vote at eighteen merely draws them a little earlier into a democratic process that seems geared to giving a mandate to the middle-aged for the running of the system according to the standards and needs of the middle classes, and particularly of their commercial interests. The apparent lack of any real and effective participation in the two forces that most shape our lives, government and industry, leads to frustration. Because public opinion is largely opposed and the working masses indifferent to the crying needs of the day, as seen by the young, the rulers can afford to remain complacent and unheeding. Self-interest appears to prevail all too frequently over generosity.

And so the young protest. More than that, they often turn to an active dislike of the age groups and classes from which they consider the oppressors to come, and of the vested interests that cause their disillusionment, insecurity and helplessness. This is true even of Christian groups. One can almost feel, for instance, the scorching antagonism burning out of every edition of *The Catonsville Roadrunner* (a paper for young and radical Christians) against 'the World Pig' (the establishment) and the 'fuzz' (or police) that protect it.

It would be beside the point to offer any justification here for these attitudes, or indeed to condemn those among the young who face up to present problems in this way. It would also be idle to assert once again that it is these very problems that help make religion attractive today, even to Christians. For we must first look at the origins and developments of religion as such if we are to see how deeply it is at variance with the teaching of Jesus Christ.

2

THE GROWTH OF RELIGION

RELIGION IS wholly the invention of the priests, who have deliberately battened upon the fears, the desires and the gullibility of ordinary folk in order to further their own ends. They have palmed off upon the people a set of superstitious fables about the gods and an after-life so as to silence their just demands for a better way of living here and now, to terrorise them into serving and providing for the priestly caste without protest, or to force them into supporting whatever power-structure the priests might approve as being of the greatest advantage to their own position.

So ran an explanation of the origins of religion that was quite popular at the turn of the century. It will not do, however, today. Not only is it too suspiciously simple an interpretation, and one that is all too plainly coloured by the nineteenth-century challenges to the establishment and the established churches, but it is almost wholly at variance with the findings of modern anthropology.

The analyses of men like Mircea Eliade have shown quite clearly that the religions of primitive people display a generally similar pattern of origin and growth. And it is one that has little or nothing to do with any crafty collusion on the part of the clergy, but that can be much more satisfactorily explained in terms of mankind's bewildered response to a largely hostile environment.

It was a response that took two main forms.

The radical insecurity men felt in an environment that they did not understand gave rise to the *creation myth* and the cult of the creator-god. The world seems to the primitive a threatening and chaotic place, the domain of change, instability, growth and decay, when what he is searching after is security, durability, *being*. So he arrives at some kind of imaginative explanation of his situation that will comfort him and convince him he has value in the midst of his seemingly impossible circumstances.

As he looks up from his changeable earthly home to the wide and changeless sky, he tends to think of the blue heavens as in fact an all-embracing, permanent deity, a father-in-the-clouds who, once upon a time, made the earth and its inhabitants and is able, even now, to give human beings a share in his own stability and richness of being. Man's search for this divine gift gave rise, therefore, to the notions of the sacred time, the sacred place and the ritual worship that went on there.

If the creator-god is to look with favour upon a man and his tribe, and grant them security by protecting them from the surrounding evils that menace their existence and are often imagined as rival deities to the sky-father and his minion-gods, then men must first win his favour and find out how to draw upon the power of his being by turning to the sacred time and place where this flowing force is especially outpoured.

The return to the *sacred time* 'in the beginning' when the god and his underlings created the world and the tribal ancestors and gave them their particular skills and accomplishments is made possible by the solemn recounting, in recitation, mime, song and dance, of the myth of creation. Particularly at the start of a new year, this return to the time of creation means, in fact, a *re*-creation of the tribe and of its abilities and occupations, which are often 'learned anew' in the annual rites. ('Plough Sunday' in this country seems to be in part a survival of this 'learning anew' when the ritual furrow is mimically drawn before the 'holy place' – now the parish church – so as to ensure a good harvest.) Just as the gods brought the world and the tribe into being 'in the beginning' out of the chaos of non-being so, after the season of misrule that frequently preceded the turn of the year, the same gods will re-form the people for what was hoped would be a twelve-month of more settled and certain an existence.

This power-of-being of the high god is not only to be met with in the sacred seasons but also at the *sacred place*. The tribal en-campment or village will generally be centred around a holy spot where some object resides that is capable of putting the people into contact with the sky-father and at the same time keeping at bay the demons of the underworld. The sacred pole or pillar, tree or altar, will be looked upon as the centre of this particular tribe's universe, with its roots firmly planted upon the evil gods down below and its tip or summit in contact with the creating deity above. It is in the sacred place and its cult-object, then, that the being of the chief god is drawn down to earth, to flow out over the whole of his people.

If the sacred place is the *umbilicus mundi*, the navel of the tribe's world, then the encampment or village will be seen as an image of that world in miniature. It will often be deliberately constructed outwards from the central shrine in the form of a cross to sym-bolise the earth's own extension when it, too, was originally formed out of a single lump and drawn outwards into the four quarters of the north, south, east and west. (It is not solely for the sake of convenience or Christian symbolism, according to Eliade, that most ancient European churches, villages and towns are constructed in this cruciform way, or built around a crossroads, with the church standing often on the site of the old holy place and thus in the central position, its steeple piercing the skies.)

However, the father-god's influence will only go as far as the edges of the tribe's settlement or the frontiers of its territories. Beyond this, all will be chaos, danger and threat. The stockade or wall around the tribal area stands for more, in consequence, than a defence against human or animal enemies. It is also the magic circle that marks the limits of the god's influence. Inside is reality and being; outside, only danger and the evils of the forest or wilderness where the devils dwell.

The house, too, was usually thought of as another sacred place, the centre-of-being for the individual family. Here, in place of today's ubiquitous TV aerial tuned in to catch its own brand of magical forces, the chimney-hole or tent-pole was thought to draw down the god's power upon the household within. And in either place, home or temple, the high-god and his underlings would be worshipped.

Although the new year observances were fundamental for the tribe's very survival, yet, when calamity threatened and the creator seemed asleep, he could be woken up and cajoled into further action on his people's behalf by means of rites he would find irresistible. These rites, performed in most primitive communities at first by the fathers of families or elders of the tribe, tended to be handed over, in time, to a particular caste of priests, who alone knew the sacred formulae or spells and the actions that should accompany them, and who were alone qualified by divine choice for performing them before the shrine of the god.

Such a worship was, of course, magical. If the correct offerings were made, the correct words spoken and the correct deeds performed the correct number of times and at the correct seasons, then the father-god was bound to be impressed. When he failed to come to his people's aid and misfortune fell upon them, this could only be because there was something lacking in the ritual performance, in the performers themselves, or in the recent activity of the tribe, which perhaps had eaten the wrong food, killed the wrong animal, gone into the wrong place or otherwise unwittingly offended.

And so a *taboo code* of morality was formed. Here, rules relating to health, hygiene and good behaviour, and obviously conducive to the well-being of the tribe, would be mixed up with purely ritual precepts and meaningless prohibitions, any of which, once broken, called out for expiation and purification. The angry god had to be placated and the law-breaker brought back into his favour if the tribe were to retain the divine friendship. This idea that the god could be automatically offended even by a purely accidental 'sin' and could in consequence be automatically placated by a purely formal piece of ceremonial is yet another feature of the magical that is to be found in primitive religions and is indeed apparent in parts of the Old Testament, in the Greek tragedies and in many of our old fairy stories.

In order to discern exactly how the god had been offended, or to see how to avoid offending him in the future, most primitive religions relied upon an *oracle* of some kind, that is, upon a chosen person or particular device through which the divine word could be relayed to the people. Thus, by poking into the smoking entrails of a slaughtered beast, by casting lots, by searching the skies for omens and portents or by listening to the often ambiguous sayings of a wise, entranced or far-sighted human seer, they believed they could discover the will of the gods.

The primitive cult of the creator-god is, then, a *magical* religion in so far as it is bound to: (1) the sacred time and place and the automatically-effective rite; (2) the ministry of a priestly caste; (3) the observance of a list of irrational taboos; and (4) the divinations of the oracle. For it seeks, by these means, to win a hold upon the deity and force from him some of his power of being.

And it is magical because it is neurotic. That is to say, it is a religion that grew up mainly because our ancestors were otherwise unable to face the fact of their own existence. The imponderables were too many, the mysteries too terrifying and the dangers too overwhelming.

The predicament that produced the creation myths and the cult of the powerful sky-god also produced the *fertility religions*. Again, the fact that primitive man depended for survival upon the fecundity not only of his wife but also of the herds he hunted, the flocks he grazed or the seed he planted, and his awareness that this productivity was constantly threatened by the apparently fickle and arbitrary forces of barrenness, disease, flood or drought, all this led to his constructing a *myth of the divine marriage* and the cult of the god and goddess of fertility.

At first, fertility was generally associated with a mother-figure, a goddess who went through a yearly metamorphosis with the seasons and was identified, in her first phase as virgin, with the moon. In the spring, however, this virgin became the earth-mother, conceiving and giving birth to all living things before departing, when grown old and barren with the year, into her wintry underworld. As man's own role in the childbearing process came to be better understood, then a mate had to be provided for the mother-goddess. And so the sun (or sometimes the sky) came to be regarded as a male god who was born anew each mid-winter and grew to manhood by the time of the spring equinox, when he would wed the moon-maiden at her descent upon the earth, warming her into fertility and life by the increasing strength of his rays. He, too, remained close to the earth until, after the glory of mid-summer, he grew progressively more frail and eventually accompanied his withered wife into the depths below.

The fertility religions were concerned with helping along this divine mating, ensuring its fruitfulness and thus gaining for a particular people and its fields and flocks an increased share of the divine fecundity. Very often, such worship would express itself in the form of a *sacred orgy*, in which certain selected men or women, the priests or priestesses, were held to be incarnations of the god or goddess, to make love with whom assured for the worshipper a further fruitful year.

And since, furthermore, the gift of fertility was a more urgent and ever-recurring requirement than rescue from destruction or deliverance from one's enemies, so the worship of the divine pair eclipsed that of the sky-god in the day-to-day living of many primitives, who would only turn to the latter when calamity actually threatened.

It was against the allurements of just such a religion, with its magical rites, hillside shrines and sacred prostitutes, that the Old Testament prophets were so constantly having to warn the Israelites, reminding them that Yahweh was not only their creator but also himself the one and only giver of life. And it was against the same kind of religion that European Christianity waged so long and discreditable a war in the past.

For the *witchcraft* of northern Europe was originally the religion of our ancestors, and as such concerned predominantly with the cult of a god and goddess of fertility.

The fertility god whom the witches worshipped, and who has had a greater impact upon our folk-lore than his divine bride, seems originally to have been a god of hunter or herdsman rather than one of field and harvest. Thus, when our ancestors passed out of a nomadic way of life and settled down to tend their flocks and plough their fields, the deity they sought to bring fertility to their work seems still to have often been pictured as one of the kinds of animal the tribe had hitherto depended upon for food and survival. Among hunting people, the stag had been frequently chosen and among herdsmen the goat, presumably because either species is more dramatic in its sexuality than its fellows, and thus represents more forcefully the fertility of quarry or flock.

In the rite that was eventually to be known as the *witches' sabbath*, the worshippers would gather round some sacred object – a tree or well, maypole or standing stone – and particularly at the holy times of mid-winter, mid-summer and the spring and autumn equinoxes, there to join in a ring-dance or *carol*, singing hymns to their god, represented by a chief priest or *wizard*, who was disguised in the skin of goat or stag the better to resemble the god whose incarnation he was held to be. Led by the *witches*, his priestesses, the people would ensure a guaranteed fertility for the coming year by taking part in an orgy, a real or mimic mating with the deity.

For propaganda purposes and to wean the people away from such unseemly worship, the Christian missionaries not only built their churches, when they could, upon the old holy places but they and their successors tried for centuries to stamp out the ring-dance, to christen the lyrics of the carol and to demote the old and potent god by identifying him with Lucifer, the enemy of Jesus. And so, in Europe, the Devil came to be depicted as the goat-god of our forefathers, and as he had for long been impersonated by wizard and warlock, that is, as a man with horns and tail and cloven hooves.

In the classical world, however, the fertility religions underwent another kind of change. With the expansion of the Roman

Empire, the Hellenistic culture upon which it came to be based made increasing contact with the fertility myths of the conquered territories, and with stories of goddesses – and particularly of gods – who died and rose every year, and who, in doing so, brought new life to their supplicants.

Such legends tended to be understood by Greek or Roman in much the same way that they were already beginning to understand the myths about their own traditional fertility gods. Dionysus, in other words, was no longer regarded as the wine-god of the vine-growing Grecian countryside or Mithras as the deity of Persian hunters and cattlemen. And the annual humiliation and exaltation of many of these deities no longer came to be interpreted as simply a way of explaining the world's apparent death each winter and its rising to new life every spring. Instead, the old stories, plus the rites that accompanied them, became the *mystery religions* that were so prevalent and popular throughout the empire in the early years of Christianity.

In each, the god revealed to his disciples the secret of how to share in his own immortality. One simply underwent the initiation ceremonies, the ritual baths or mimic burials that signified one's identity with the god in his lowliness, and the ceremonial raising-up that signified one's identity with him in his state of exaltation.

From now on, and no matter how remiss the quality of one's own personal life might be, one was safe and secure since a partaker in the everlasting life of the victorious god. Furthermore, this saving contact could be deepened and an increased share of the god's glory infallibly gained by means of communion rites in the form of sacred sacrifices, meals or orgies.

In other words, the mystery religions were as much religions of *magic* as the fertility cults out of which they sprang. They worked automatically and gave the worshipper guaranteed divine power. For, whatever his own private dispositions, once he had undergone the initiation rites he was inevitably at one with the god in his exalted condition; hence the great secrecy that often surrounded the sacred words and actions. The mystery was not to be shared with all and sundry, but was reserved for a chosen élite, for the privileged few.

If these mystery cults represent a Graeco-Roman refinement of the fertility religions of the Mediterranean basin, so the same culture's view of the surrounding world represents in great part a refinement of the old myths of creation. In this case, however, the sky, instead of giving rise to the picture of an immortal father-god on high, becomes the philosophical idea of *spirit*, or of an enduring reality that contrasts sharply with the ever-changing *matter* out of which this earth is apparently composed, a reality that indeed gives to the material world what little durability and value it has.

This world of matter that makes itself known to us through our senses is thus but the pale shadow of some spiritual counterpart in the realm of ideas, or else it reveals to us the underlying, non-material principle that gives to the things we thus see or taste or handle their form and reality.

And the wise man, whose own powers of thinking have been purified and set free from the distorting influence of sensual demands by asceticism and right living, is able, through *meditation*, to make contact with this spiritual reality that gives a transient existence to the unstable objects of this world. He is thus able to discern the *divine order* that lies behind or beyond our universe, and, in its light, to direct more accurately the life of the spiritual soul that is either imprisoned within his flesh and bones or else that gives reality to his body and makes of him a human being.

This classical esteem for the man of wisdom gave rise to an opinion, current in the Graeco-Roman world in the first two to three centuries of Christianity, that the man who courageously lived by the knowledge his sharpened intellect rightly perceived would himself become divine. By struggling heroically to live up to his ideals, he would gradually grow into a *son of God*. And it would not be too far-fetched to make out, working behind this cult of the godlike man, a vague memory of the life-giving gods of fertility whom folk-lore had already begun to demote into merely human heroes or to transform into the gods of the mysteries.

Five hundred years before the coming of Jesus, the religion of the Persian sage *Zoroaster* had already combined the two ideas of wisdom and of the divine hero into the doctrine of a saviour who as to come at the end of time to bring resurrection and new life to 'the followers of the Truth' (as revealed to Zoroaster), and a fiery doom to 'the followers of the Lie' (those who clung to the tenets of the older religion of Persia).

The same kind of ideas grew up in Judaism, so that by the time of Christ the *anthropos* and *sophia* myths were widely current. The anthropos myth told how Adam, the first man, had come down from heaven in the beginning; the sophia myth spoke of the wisdom of God as though it were a person who came down to earth at the moment of creation (and through whom all things were made) but who was rejected by men and so returned to God.

At this period, another religion – or rather an amalgam of many classical and near-eastern philosophies and religions – had started to spread through the empire and was eventually to prove a strong rival to the gospel itself. This was the system known as *gnosticism*.

Although there is some dispute today about the extent to which the gnostics of New Testament times had fully articulated their myth of a *fallen redeemer*, or indeed whether such a myth may not have been largely the product of over-speculative German theologians of our own century, we will assume, for our present purposes, that men like Käsemann are right and the full-blown myth did in fact exist among them.

To understand something of the origins of gnosticism, we must first recognise that, in many creation stories, the good sky-god was only able to construct our world after fighting with an evil god who ever sought to destroy his handiwork. Sometimes, as in the myths of Babylon, the earth itself was seen as the body of this evil deity, slain by the creator in the beginning. For the Persians, the good god, with his legions of angels, was perpetually at war with a god of evil and with his hordes of demons who strove to lay hold upon this world.

Gnosticism took ideas like these one stage further and asserted that *matter itself* was evil – so evil, indeed, that it would be demeaning to think of the supreme deity, who dwelt in the spirit-world above, sullying his purity by creating the earth directly. Instead, it was the work of a fallen, lesser god, a *demi urge*, who again sounds like a faint echo of the old fertility gods in their relationship with the sky-father.

It was the demi urge who imparted to his chosen disciples, by means of a whole range of inferior spirits who were gradually less and less spiritual and more and more earthy according to their position in the hierarchy, the secret and saving *knowledge* as to how their spiritual souls might escape from the material world and from their own bodies in order to ascend, step by step, through all the degrees of the spirit-world until they arrived at the supreme god himself. In fact, the ascent was to be made by the use of arcane rites and formulae every bit as magical as those of the mystery cults.

The same trend towards the despising of matter can be traced in the story of Hinduism as it developed out of the primitive fertility religions of the Indian sub-continent. We find, for example, after the Aryan or Indo-European invasions of about four thousand years ago, the cult of a new god known as 'Sky-father' or '*Dyaus-pitar*', whose very name reveals the original meaning of the Latin '*Deus pater*'.

Hinduism began, however, gradually to rarify this idea. *Dyaus-pitar* came to be replaced, by the time of the *Vedas* or early hymns to the gods, by *Varuna*, and he in his turn gave way, as we see from the *Brahmanas* or books of priestly ritual compiled between 1000 and 600 B.C., to the great Lord of Production, *Prajapati*. Finally, at the beginning of the Christian era, *Vishnu* had come to the fore as the chief of all the gods. Thus he is the central figure of the *Bhagavad-gita* and other epic poems, and is known as the protector of *Rama*, by now the great hero of Hinduism, and as having been incarnated in the Lord *Krishna*.

Meanwhile, the *Upanishads* (700–500 B.C.), a series of intricate theological dialogues, had introduced a significant refinement in the notion of *Brahman* and *Atman*. For they teach that *Brahman* is all. *Brahman* is the impersonal force, that is to say, that sustains all things, is in all things, underlies all things, so much so that anything other than *Brahman*, including the whole of the material world, is mere *maya* or illusion. But the breath of *Brahman* is *Atman*, or the human soul. And *Brahman* and *Atman* are one.

Indeed, it is only by becoming deeply aware of this *Brahman/Atman* unity in himself that a man can find liberation from the chains of *maya* and from the endless cycle of successive reincarnations, the *samsara* in which he is otherwise inevitably involved.

He may seek to do good, to love his neighbour. But this, the way of *karma*, can never win him deliverance. Either he will fail in his task, thus increasing his guilt and condemning himself to inhabit some lower form when his present body dies, or he will convince himself that he is actually achieving something worthwhile and positive in his pursuit of the good life. But such a conviction can only be false, for the world of matter in which, by his deeds, he is involving himself, has no real existence.

Again, he may follow the path of devotion, or *bhakti*. He may take up the chanting of *mantras* in praise of the gods and thus automatically win blessings for the earth. But *Vishnu*, who makes himself manifest in *Krishna* and the other gods, is himself supported by the formless power that is *Brahman*. To venerate a mere god or 'formed Brahman' is therefore to miss the true mark.

For the only way to find *mukti*, or the release of the soul from the reincarnation process by its reabsorption into *Brahman*, is the way of *yoga*. Far from being simply an aid to slimming or to mental health, this technique of meditation opens out (to those with the courage – or fate – to accept it) the certainty of saving enlightenment. It alone is able to help a man pay less and less heed to the illusion of matter, teaching him to reject all activity, whether good or bad, and to leave aside devotion to the gods so as to focus all his attention on the fact that *Brahman* is everything and that he, in his *Atman*, is *Brahman*. Once this stage is reached, the *yogi* need fear no further incarnation. His death will liberate him from the coils of matter.

Thus the pious Hindu is intended to divide up his own life into four stages. In the first, he works as a student, studying the *Vedas* under a *guru* or teacher. In the second, he takes up the normal domestic life of a householder, a family man. Next, he is meant to become a wandering hermit and lead an ascetical life alone in the jungle. In the last stage, if he perseveres thus far, he will achieve a saving union with *Brahman* through his own increased abstinence, self-control and meditations.

Buddhism took the Hindu refinement of the old sky-god religion a good deal further and, with greater pessimism, asserted that the notion of *maya* extends even to the concepts of *Brahman* and self.

Gautama, later to become the *Buddha*, was born in India, near Benares, in about 560 B.C. As a young man, he became very much preoccupied with the unpalatable fact that all human beings must suffer the pains of birth, sickness, old age and death. So, at the age of twenty-nine, he left wife and children to take up the third and fourth stages of the Hindu way and become an ascetic. For seven years he tried, by the most rigorous self-discipline, to rid himself of *karma* and thus win *mokti*, his release from the ever-turning wheel of *samsara* in which most men are trapped.

Emancipation finally came. But with it came enlightenment, and the sure knowledge that the traditional teachings of Hinduism were inadequate. Thus, while sitting cross-legged under the bo-tree at Buddh Gaya, did Gautama, after seven days, become the *Buddha*, or enlightened one.

He saw that extravagant asceticism led as much as did the excessive pursuit of good works to an increase of *karma* and not the reverse. For it made one more conscious of one's self, and more concerned about one's liberation. But self, for the Buddha, did not exist. What men call self is merely a succession of impressions they receive day by day, and that are themselves *maya* or illusion. To pay heed to such impressions, to treat them as real, to think of them as proving the reality of one's own ego, is to be deceived by *maya*. More than that, it is to prevent one's liberation.

For it is *karma*, or the actions we take in our anxiety to avoid suffering and to survive as individuals, that keeps us bound down in the web of matter. It is *karma*, not our self-hood, that survives death. It is *karma* that condemns us to inhabit other bodies when we die, and thus begin our sufferings anew.

For the Buddha, the only way out was to rid one's self of *karma* by rejecting the very notion of self. Thus, in the *Four Noble Truths*, he taught that, though all men suffer in this life, yet the cause of their sufferings is their frantic and desperate desire for an illusory personal existence. How, then, can such suffering be avoided? Plainly, by ridding oneself of self, by a passive and quietist recognition that pain is unreal, since the self that seems to feel pain is in fact non-existent. Such a state of selflessness can only be achieved, however, by following the *Eightfold Path* of correct understanding, behaviour, resolution, speech, occupation, effort, meditation and concentration.

The *Eightfold Path*, which really means living, acting and thinking more and more in accord with the principle that matter, suffering and self have no reality, will lead to that *Higher Wisdom* that brings with it peace, insight and *Nirvana*.

Nirvana, the state of blessedness when all *karma* is gone, all effort ceases and the illusion of selfhood has faded away, may be reached even in this life, in which case one enters, after death, into that state in its fullness, into *Parinirvana*.

It follows, therefore, that only the monk can attain to *Nirvana*, since ordinary folk can have neither time nor opportunity to pursue the later stages of the *Eightfold Path*, and cannot give their lives over to perpetual meditation and concentration. Thus both the stricter form of Buddhism, the *Hinayana* or *Lesser Vehicle*, and the more lax *Greater Vehicle* or *Mahayana*, agree that the monk is a man who, in past incarnations, has so successfully divested himself of *karma* that he has deserved this his present destiny, one that has placed him on the very threshold of *Nirvana*.

(Such are the ideas, in fact, that lie behind *Zen* Buddhism, so popular in certain circles in the United States and differentiated from other forms by its particular theory of meditation, based upon the notion that enlightenment arises best out of the unexpected, the surprising, the illogical.)

Hinduism combined with its teachings on *maya* a strong belief in the power of magic. Indeed, even today the sun only rises, apparently, and the seasons only change because the priests, the *brahmans*, are saying the correct spells and making the correct sacrifices. And if it should seem to us strange that a religion so anti-materialistic in theory should find room in its system for methods of controlling the universe by superstitious means, then it is perhaps even stranger to discover that Buddhism has also, from the earliest times, contained a strongly magical element.

Though the Buddhist *Tantra*, with its stated aims not only of showing the reader how to gain enlightenment but also how to win health, wealth and power by means of magic, dates only from the sixth century A.D., it is nevertheless the elaboration of traditions that go back to the beginnings of the movement, and indeed, *via* Hinduism, to the primitive religions of India. In the *Tantra* writings, along with lofty doctrines about *Nirvana* and the non-reality of our world, our bodies and our selves, we find, for example, the *mantra* advocated, in all its forms, as a spell of remarkable power; we find the use of the magic circle, called in Buddhism the *mandala*; we find devotion to the saints or *bodhi-sattvas* of Buddhism and the gods of Hinduism (represented more as powers than as people) spoken of as a way of gaining one's own ends in this life; we find images venerated because charged with magical energy; we find the old mother-goddess of India become the *Mother of all the Buddhas*, and worshipped as source of fertility; we find secret rites of initiation into the practice of magic; and we even find the doctrine proclaimed that this practice will guarantee one's becoming an enlightened one in turn, a *buddha* or *bodhisattva*.

In our survey of the more important religious movements that were flourishing among the interrelated peoples of India and the Graeco-Roman world at the time of Jesus, we have come to recognise how these have developed, with the progress of civilisation, out of very similar kinds of belief in the gods of creation and fertility.

B

Civilisation grew up with the cities. That is to say, it was only when wandering tribes were able to settle down as fixed communities that lived no longer by hunting or by following the herd, but by farming, tilling and pasturing, that they had the leisure and the breathing-space to make a start on those pursuits that were to produce the ancient cultures of Asia, the near east or the classical world.

It is not surprising that the beliefs and ideas of such people about human existence – as we find them expressed in the mystery religions, for example, in Hinduism, or in Buddhist or Hellenistic thought – should be *cyclic*. For they were largely sophisticated adaptations of the outlook of the farmer, who tends to see the history of the world in the same way that he sees the round of the seasons, as one great, ever-turning and ever-recurring wheel. And, in seeking to explain the meaning behind such a view of existence, the ancient religions and philosophies sought either to reconcile men to the process, to give them power over it or to show them how they might escape it.

Later civilisations, or those with stronger roots in their more distant, nomadic past, will tend to see things differently. For them, life will be a *progress*, a journey to some future home in which the seasonal cycle will merely mark the stages along the way. Thus their cast of thought will tend to be concerned, not so much with *order* as with *development*, and their religions less with the *epiphany* of the god, or his revelation of the hidden meaning behind a world caught up in the exhausting wheel of time, but with the divine *eschaton*, the goal that is held out to man by his god at the end of the pilgrimage.

It follows that Judaism, and hence the faiths of Christianity and Islam and the Marxist ideology that sprang from it, will be of the eschatological rather than the epiphany type, more concerned with looking forward to the future of the world than with escaping from it into some ideal or purely spiritual realm. In this sense, as we shall see, the religion of the Old Testament, as it drew away from the false security of the magical flight from the real world, prepared the way for the coming of Jesus, who fulfilled Judaism precisely by eradicating from it all that was left of the magical and presenting, instead, a faith that runs clean contrary to the basic tenets of the old religions of creation and fertility.

3

THE ANTI-RELIGION

1. The Religious Climate in Jesus's Day

EVER SINCE their return from Babylon some five hundred years before the birth of Jesus, the Jewish people had displayed a growing uneasiness with the magical elements that still remained in their religion. Their experiences in exile, and especially their unexpected and almost miraculous escape back to Palestine, had convinced them that God had been with them despite their long separation from the holy-of-holies and its sacrifices. Hence, their piety tended to focus upon the presence of the Lord among his people wherever they might be – with the family gathered for worship in the home or with the local community met together in the synagogue – rather than with his presence in one particular sacred spot.

By the time of Christ, the Jews had come to regard as their greatest yearly sacrificial feast the meal of the Passover that was basically a family affair celebrated in the domestic dining-room and presided over by the head of the household. Likewise, the synagogue was becoming so important a place of worship that Judaism was quite well able to survive the destruction of its temple and the cult of the sanctuary in A.D. 70.

Again, though the Jewish code of morality was hailed as the law of Moses that had been dictated by God, yet there was much disagreement at this period as to what that law actually required of the Jew. While the Pharisees were all for extending it and interpreting it most severely, the Sadducees and others were for restricting it and making it more reasonable and easy of observance. There was, furthermore, a growing reluctance to admit that the law could be broken unwittingly and God thereby offended inadvertently.

Indeed, this resistance to the idea that the will of God could be spelled out in some sort of taboo code or that Yahweh could be automatically placated by the performance of magical rites in the temple stemmed in large measure from meditation upon the words of the great prophets who had lived around the time of the exile. Again and again, they had insisted that the only worship that is really pleasing to the Lord is a man's free offering of his own heart, and that thus to donate one's life to God's service by loving one's neighbour is to obey the fundamental requirements of the law. And the Jews were beginning to listen.

Not that it was easy or pleasant to hear and take notice of the words of the prophets. A religion based upon the automatically effective rite in the holy place and upon the observance of a taboo code is far less demanding than one based upon personal commitment. As Martin Buber puts it (*The Eclipse of God*, New York, 1955), 'The prophets of Israel have never announced a God with whom their hearers' striving for security reckoned. They have always aimed to shatter all security and to proclaim in the opened abyss of the final insecurity the unwished-for God who demands that his human creatures become real, become human, and confounds all who imagine that they can take refuge in the certainty that the temple of God is in their midst.'

The prophets, then, relayed the word of their God not as seers or oracles might have done, that is, by delivering some highly ambiguous message about an individual's inescapable fate, but as men compelled to throw out a challenge to their kinsfolk by promising them a blessed future as God's People only if they were prepared to commit themselves to creating that future here and now instead of avoiding it by escaping into magic.

The written word of God, the bible of first century Judaism that was made up of the books of the Law, the Prophets and the Writings and that had only begun to take on its final form after the exile, proclaimed the same message. Though it made much use of folk-lore and legend that was often magical in tone, and of the language and imagery of the pagan myths, it nevertheless represented, in many of its more important themes, a refinement of more primitive religious ideas. This is particularly evident in its treatment of creation and the gift of life.

Although Genesis presents us with the picture of a creator-God that is largely derived from the myths of Canaan and Babylon, yet it is a picture with a difference. For here we find no rivalry between good and evil deities. Rather, the one God and his handiwork are both supremely good, and wickedness proceeds instead from out of the heart of man.

For the serpent whom we find tempting Eve and then, through her, Adam, in the Genesis account of creation and the fall based upon the myths of Canaan (chapter 2, beginning at verse 5, and chapter 3), is no god of wickedness himself. Rather, he is a symbol, standing for everything that the good Israelite ought to detest. For it was a common thing among the pagan peoples of the ancient near east to represent their gods of fertility, the *baalim* against whose worship the prophets protested so vigorously, as snakes, very often associating them with trees, the greenwood tree being itself a powerful image of life. Indeed, the custom was wider than that, according to the anthropologists. D. H. Lawrence, after all, was not the first, in his poem *Snake*, to see the serpent as a phallic symbol and one of the lords of life, for the tree-and-snake motif is very widespread and primitive, figuring in the fertility cults of Java, for example.

And worship of the snake-god took the form of the sacred orgy, with the men coupling with shrine or temple prostitutes. Hence the basic truth in the saying of the prophets that the Israelite who frequented the hillside shrines of the baalim around Jerusalem was guilty of adultery; and hence, indeed, the obvious sexual overtones to the biblical story of the fall.

For the writer is taking hold of the worst sin he can think of, the involvement by a servant of God in the cult of the serpent, and presenting it as the very type of all that is evil. He is not, in other words, saying that sex itself is tainted or regrettable, nor that man's first offence was sexual in nature. Neither is he accusing womankind in general of invariably tempting the male into sin. Instead, he is using the story of Eve, the woman, leading her husband, Adam, astray as an illustration of those times in Jewish history when the kings married pagan brides who introduced the cult of the snake-baal among the People of God.

For the king, Yahweh's viceroy and vicar, to encourage or at least permit the worship of pagan deities is the sorriest example the writer of Genesis can imagine of a man's fall into sin. And he makes use of it, therefore, to illustrate the fact that all sin comes, not from God, but from human beings themselves.

The serpent, then, is not to be regarded as having individual existence, any more than the pagan gods he stands for were held by the writer to have real existence. He is simply the symbol of the evil that mankind finds attractive. He cannot, therefore, be identified with Satan or the Devil, for, though Christians have wrongly made this identification in the past, the Jews have never done so, nor do they today.

And despite its use of the old imagery of a God who lives in the sky and who goes back to bed after he has finished creating, yet Genesis is not really concerned with filling its readers with a nostalgic yearning for the paradise that existed in the sacred time at the beginning of the world, but with spurring them on to finding and creating that paradise in the future. For the God of the Old Testament is not a deity who seeks to lead men back to a golden age in the past, but to lead them on to a golden age that is yet to come. He is a God of promise.

He is a God, in other words, of the living future and not of the dead past. And so it is he, and not any lesser pair of male and female deities, who gives life and fertility to his creation. Just as Yahweh is responsible at any given moment for the existence of the world, so he is responsible for its fecundity and its future.

God promises life. That is, he holds out the certain hope to his People that a time is coming when he shall send a messenger, a Messiah, a Christ, to deliver them fully from their slavery to evil and to inaugurate an era when Yahweh shall truly reign, both in Jerusalem and throughout the world. For in those days a new temple shall arise out of which the Spirit of eternal life shall pour to water the earth and to dwell as a new Law in the hearts of men, guiding and directing their lives from within.

2. Jesus and Judaism

Jesus of Nazareth, so his followers claimed, was precisely this Messiah, with whose coming the Last Times were finally upon us.

And Jesus opposed religion. That is to say, he fulfilled Judaism precisely by purging it of the religious elements it had inherited from its more primitive ancestry.

For, as our analysis has already shown, the religions of mankind developed by way of the myths of creation and fertility out of a response to the frightening facts of human existence that was basically, if not inevitably, neurotic, unrealistic and escapist. And, although Jesus too offered us a way of escape, it was not by showing us how to leave behind our human condition in mystical flight or to better it by the aid of magical forces. Instead, he himself shared that condition in order to transform it by stripping it of all its limitations until it reached its perfection in his rising from the dead.

In doing so, he showed us how we too might change our own humanity not by running away from it but by realising it more fully and freeing it from every let or hindrance until we in our turn should finally share, with the whole material universe, in the complete freedom that Jesus now enjoys in the kingdom of his Father, where there is neither death nor decay nor any kind of barrier to full human living.

By his life, death and resurrection, therefore, Jesus revealed to us what it was to be truly human, and made plain to us both our own and the whole world's future as fully given over, in his Spirit, to God the all-in-all.

This, at least, is the way we tend to understand his saving work today. But are we really justified in claiming that Jesus himself sought to eradicate from the Jewish faith all that smacked of the old religion of the creation myths, with its talk of an angry sky-god, its holy places, its sacred times, its priestly caste, its powerful sacrifices, its taboo morality, its inspired oracles and the blessings of tribal security it sought to win?

If we look at the New Testament evidence – and particularly to Acts, Paul and John – we must at least agree that this is how the Christian church soon came, though not without a bitter struggle, to interpret the mind of its founder.

Oscar Cullmann has pointed out the strength of the temptation, among those early Christians whose culture was as Jewish as their origins, to keep the gospel restricted within the confines of Judaism, and the depth of the conflict and tension between them and those Jewish converts whose culture was more Greek, or Hellenistic.

Not that the tension was peculiarly Christian. Whereas the Jew from Jerusalem looked to the temple as the centre of his religious life, already the Greek-speaking Jews of the dispersion, scattered as they were among the cities of the Roman Empire, were focusing their attention more on the synagogue in their own town and beginning to criticise the whole temple set-up as a wasteful anachronism. If their forefathers had been able to survive without a temple during their exile in Babylon, they themselves could very well do the same!

At the same time, religious fanatics, particularly from Galilee, had for some time been predicting with joy the downfall of temple and priesthood, while sects like the Pharisees and Essenes habitually criticised the Sadducees who administered the temple as lax and lacking in zeal.

But Cullman would further contend – in his essay *Dissension within the Early Church* (*New Testament Issues*, ed. R. Batey, S.C.M., 1970), for example – that, beneath the idealised portrait of the early Church presented in Acts, one can detect serious conflict between the two parties that Luke calls the Judaisers and the Hellenists.

It is obvious by the time of Stephen's arrest (chapter 6) how important James the brother of the Lord is becoming. And his importance grows. Not only does he loom very large in the council of Jerusalem but also, after Peter's departure, seems to dominate the group of apostles who care for the church in Jerusalem.

Cullmann also points out how, in Romans 15, 'Paul tells us that he is going to Jerusalem in order to bring what had been received for this collection to the church there. But we do not generally give enough attention to the *fear* which the apostle expresses in this passage, fear lest that collection be refused by the leaders of the church in Jerusalem.' For Paul, the giving and receiving of the money he had gathered was a sign of unity. Yet he doubted whether or not James would accept it – so much so that we read in Acts 21:17, 18 that he goes first to his own particular friends among the Christians in Jerusalem, Hellenist like himself, and puts off facing James and the Judaisers until the next day. Why was this?

It was because Paul was a universaliser, the apostle to the gentiles. Like Peter, he saw the Christian gospel as a message meant for all men, not merely for Jews. And, though tender-hearted towards the over-scrupulous, he believed that the Law, with its precepts about circumcision and temple-worship, had come to an end. It is strange, when we recall the ferocity of his language to the Galatians who are still clinging to the old Law, to read in Acts 21:20–26 of his worshipping in the same temple, and even taking a vow and undergoing a form of penance, all to persuade James and his party of his own devotion to that Law!

And it is doubly strange when we read the speech of Stephen in chapter 7. The whole point of this highly stylised sermon is to state quite unequivocally that the temple, the priesthood, the sacrifices and the Law are all of them over and done, having been swept away by the coming of Jesus. Even before Paul's conversion, therefore, and apparently to his own knowledge, there were Christians in Jerusalem who interpreted the gospel message in these extremist terms.

Cullmann, in fact, holds the core of this extremist group to have been 'the seven', who he feels were the real leaders of the Hellenists but whom Luke, in an effort to paper over the cracks in the image of the early Church, demotes to the status of mere waiters. As for 'the twelve', these, he holds, were, with the exceptions of Peter and of James the son of Zebedee, Judaisers all, ultimately to be dominated by James the brother of the Lord. And it is certainly true, according to Luke's account of Peter's vision in the house of Cornelius, that the apostle believed Christianity to be open to all, though he also seems – perhaps out of fear of offending James and the rest of the twelve? – to have gone back on his earlier conviction and earned Paul's rebuke on that account.

'It is striking,' Cullmann goes on, 'that Luke, in Acts 12:2, is so cursory in the attention he gives the martyrdom of James,' the son of Zebedee. 'He gives it six words! It is, after all, a question of the very first martyr among the twelve apostles. Is not the explanation for such a truncated reference once again Luke's tendency to present the early Christians as perfectly united? Is not this brevity inspired by the desire to cloak in silence the difference existing between the attitude of James, son of Zebedee, and of Peter, on the one hand, and that of James, the brother of Jesus, and the other apostles, on the other hand? Indeed, James and Peter alone are persecuted. James is put to death, and Peter after his deliverance had to depart from Jerusalem and leave the supervision of the community to James, Jesus' brother, and the other apostles.'

In the long run, it is the interpretation of Jesus' message put forward by Peter, Stephen and Paul that holds the day. Jerusalem was destroyed by the Romans in A.D. 70, and with it not only did the temple disappear but also the community of Judaising Christians, so that, by the time the gospel of John comes to be written, the author can present Jesus as himself openly foretelling the destruction of that temple with all its observances and claiming himself to be the one true holy place where men may meet their God, the only real priest who can worship the Father on our behalf, the unique sacrificial offering for the sins of the world, the full Word and Law of a loving and indwelling God who comes in the Spirit of love to inaugurate the Last Times.

The blessed future, therefore, that Jesus calls his followers to pursue and asks to help him bring about by their own self-

sacrificial lives consists neither in their political triumph over
other tribes or societies, nor their escape into some fairy-like and
'sacred' time or realm beyond or outside the material universe,
but is precisely the transfiguration of this their everyday world
into the kingdom of the Father, when the whole of creation shall
enjoy the glory of its risen Lord. Only then shall God's act of
creation have reached its completion and the resurrection of Jesus
its fulfilment in a future that is already on its way and is certain of
eventual achievement.

But if we say that Christ alone is mankind's true and only
Word, temple, priest, sacrifice, law and future, we must nevertheless remember that it is metaphorical language we are using
here. It would be dangerous, in consequence, to understand such
terms as claiming, for instance, that all other systems of priesthood
and sacrifice are but imperfect manifestations and pale shadows of
the one authentic priest and sacrifice, Jesus Christ. Rather, the
terminology of the old religion of the creator-god, as this had
filtered through into Judaism, furnished the first Jewish believers
in Christianity with the only language they could meaningfully
use when attempting to describe to their fellow-countrymen something of the import and uniqueness of this man's life and death.
In other words, it is the priests and sacrifices of paganism and of
the Old Testament that are the genuine articles, and Jesus and his
work are described as such only by analogy, and then only
effectively in a world and culture that knows at first hand of cult
and shrine and ritual slaughter.

Ernst Käsemann puts this rather well when he reminds us, in
Jesus Means Freedom (London, 1969), that 'we ought to keep in
mind that today the word *sacrifice* is used and understood only in
relation to an outstanding, and indeed heroic, performance. No
one can be interested in pushing Jesus into the realm of the heroic;
that must not be done in any circumstances. On the other hand,
however, we are faced with the difficulty that we in our kind of
civilisation no longer practise cultic sacrifices; at best we simply
know of them historically, and at worst we associate them with
ideas of magic. What is more, all these sacrifices are intended to

elicit God's favour by a pious deed. That is true, even of the Old Testament, although they are explained by divine initiative and gracious permission. In regard to these, too, the New Testament declares that God reconciles himself with us, and cannot be reconciled by us through any human act. As long as the practice of offering sacrifices was openly maintained by Jews and Gentiles, one could say, as in Hebrews, 'That has been surpassed, fulfilled and finally ended by Jesus.' Today such a comparison has lost its compelling force, because our environment does not give us the direct practice of sacrificial offerings. Only the initiated can supply them from their knowledge of the Old Testament.'

3. Jesus and the Mystery Gods

If the New Testament borrows some of its terms from the old religion of the creation myths and applies them only analagously to the career of Jesus of Nazareth, it will be in order to deprive that religion of its own power and significance for man's destiny. And this same process can be seen to be at work with regard to the fertility cults and to their extensions into Judaism, the mystery religions and Hellenistic and Gnostic speculations about the divine hero and redeemer.

In fact, the fertility religions never took the same kind of hold upon the faith of the Jews as did the cult of the creator. It is true that the temptation to turn to the harvest deities of their farming neighbours seems to have been felt by the Hebrews almost as soon as they settled down in Palestine. But such a procedure came increasingly to be viewed as a betrayal of the God who had saved them. This was particularly so after the exile, when it was the more clearly realised that Yahweh was, in fact, the one and only God of Jew and Gentile alike.

It was in this post-exilic period, therefore, that we find the Palestinian feasts of fertility being widely reinterpreted by the Jews before being taken up into their own liturgical cycle.

Thus the ancient spring rites of their nomadic, sheep-rearing ancestors, in which a lamb used to be killed and eaten and its blood smeared on the tent-pole to ensure a successful lambing season, came to be combined with the sacred meal in which the people of Canaan, in the company of their gods, ate loaves of unleavened bread that had been prepared from the first sheaves of the new barley harvest. The feast of Passover that resulted no longer sought, in a magical way, to win a productive new year from the Lord, but instead celebrated the new life he gave to his People when first he led them out, like sheep, from their bondage in Egypt and into the fertile farmlands of Palestine.

Again, Pentecost, instead of remaining merely an early-summer feast of first-fruits, became a liturgical commemoration of the promulgation of the Law out in the desert. It was no longer a time, in other words, for trying to induce Yahweh to give an abundant harvest by thanking him for its promising beginnings, but for praising him for having, through his servant Moses, made known his will to the Hebrews above all other nations, thus choosing them for his own particular People. This was indeed the start of God's mighty harvesting, the action that assured the Jews that, some day, he would reap and gather to himself a human harvest out of all the peoples of the earth.

Indeed, the rabbis had embellished the biblical accounts by the time of Jesus in order to stress this very point. They claimed that Moses had not only climbed the holy mountain to receive the law but had actually been taken up into heaven from its tip to meet Yahweh face to face, and that, as he came down again, glowing with the reflection of God's glory, to meet the elders of Israel, so the light departed from him to hover in tongues of flame over their own heads. Immediately, they began proclaiming the newly-given law in every language known to man.

This theme of language and the gift of tongues was very important, for, just as, in the story of the tower of Babel, the different languages of mankind are meant to symbolise the deep divisions men have wrought in the race by their own evildoing, so the legend of the gift of tongues is meant to herald Babel's undoing and the beginning, through Israel, of Yahweh's plan of drawing the whole human race together again under his own lordship.

Finally, the feast of Tabernacles, though still a festival of harvest-home in which the Jewish menfolk, having camped out in the fields for the reaping, now thanked the Lord, in rites of fire and water, for the sun and rain that had made their garnering possible, had also taken on a deeper meaning. It had become, in Jesus' day, a time for thanking God for the gift of water from the rock that had kept their forefathers alive when they had lived as wandering tent-dwellers out in the parching desert. It had become a time, too, for remembering with gratitude the rains and summer sunshine that had given them their very first harvest in the land of promise and so had enabled them to exchange their nomadic way of life and their temporary encampments for a settled existence in more substantial dwellings. And it had ultimately become a time for looking forward to the mighty outpouring of the Holy Spirit, which was to flow out as the water of life eternal from the great rock on which the temple was built when the true Messiah should appear. In this sense, Tabernacles was a feast of hope that manifested the Jewish longing for the completion of the saving work that Yahweh was accomplishing, through them, for all the world.

It is one of the fundamental themes of the New Testament that Jesus himself fulfilled Passover, Pentecost and Tabernacles. That is to say, the harvest-feasts were even further removed from their religious origins in the cults of fertility by their being used in scripture as metaphors the better to describe the meaning of Christ's own life and actions.

Jesus is the Passover. In the spring of the year, he passes over from death to new life; he leaves behind the bondage of Egypt that is his enslavement to our human limitations, to temptation, suffering and death itself, and comes to enjoy a life of full and perfect freedom in the land or the Father. And, in so doing, he begins to set his People free. The blood that he shed, as lamb of God, on the cross not only wins resurrection for himself – it also enables his followers to escape the doom of everlasting banishment from the Father's home. The angel of death passes them by.

Jesus is the Pentecostal lawgiver. Luke and Acts bring out this notion so clearly that the Christian Church has traditionally and in its liturgy divided up the one mystery of the exaltation of Jesus according to the pattern to be found in these two books.

Whereas the exaltation is described in the gospels as a series of events – Christ's rising, his appearances, his gift of the Spirit – that all apparently take place on the same day, with only some editions of Mark adding a brief ascension account, Acts describes very explicitly, first, how the risen Jesus went up into heaven from a holy mountain like a new Moses, and then how, from heaven and aglow with glory, he sent down the new law, his Holy Spirit, in tongues of fire upon the elders of the new Israel, the Christian community, who at once began to proclaim in every language under heaven the content of this law – that Christ is risen from the dead, and that we, if we would share his glory, must die to our sins and model our lives henceforth on his. By the time he comes to write Acts, Luke sees, in the exaltation of Jesus, the truth that, through the presence of the Spirit on our earth, Christ seeks to gather into his Father's kingdom a single harvest out of all humanity and to unite the whole of this divided race in the bonds of fellowship. And the first-fruits of this harvesting is that little community of disciples that is bound together and with God by the Spirit of Jesus that is in its midst.

Jesus fulfils the feast of Tabernacles. According to John, he cries out in the temple on the last and greatest day of the feast that he is really the rock on which the new temple is to be built. Furthermore, having been struck by the lance of death, he will pour out the waters of the Spirit, his own risen life, upon his followers and the world. In other words, with the rising of the Saviour from the tomb, the Last Times have truly arrived; yet they will not find their completion until this Spirit flows through the heart of every human being, when the whole race shall have become one vast temple made of living stones, knit on to the Christ-rock and to one another by the love of Jesus and built up to the praise and glory of his Father. Then and only then shall the harvest be complete and mankind's pilgrimage in search of the Promised Land be finally at an end.

We have seen how, outside Judaism, the fertility cults either lingered on as witchcraft or developed into the mystery religions that were so popular in Hellenistic circles in New Testament times. Indeed, the New Testament seems to borrow quite heavily from them itself. This may be said especially of Paul, who was frequently accused by critics earlier in the century of having turned Jesus of Nazareth into just such a mystery deity.

The similarities are obvious. The mysteries speak of a revelation, the making known of a way of salvation to initiates which tells them how their god rose from the dead in ancient times and is now in heaven, and goes on to explain how his devotees may share in his exalted state, both now and for ever, if they will undergo the rites of entry into his cult (often taking the form of a mimic burial and rising, like a plunge into water or a descent into a pit) and will afterwards take part in the eating and drinking of sacred communion meals.

And yet, there is a great difference. For, though Paul will naturally speak the kind of religious language his Gentile hearers best understand, it will be in order to translate into terms that mean something to them a gospel that had nevertheless come to him, the zealous Pharisee, primarily as the completion and finalisation of the biblical faith of his own Jewish forebears.

As Wolfhart Pannenberg puts it, in his renowned work *Jesus, God and Man* (London, 1968), 'Paul could express the redeeming work of Jesus most vividly by means of the analogy between the death of Jesus and that of a mystery deity. Like a mystery deity, Jesus shared men's fate, the consequence of their sin (Rom. 6:10), and in return men receive a share in his life. That which is experienced by the Saviour has validity for those who belong to him; he lives out their fate. In this sense, Paul presented the universal vicarious significance of the death of Jesus Christ *for his time*. Today such an explanation is no longer possible. The ideas of the mystery religions can no longer be presupposed as universally convincing truth.

In contrast, *the Pauline concern to demonstrate the relation between sin and death as holding good for all humanity retains its validity today*. . . . No one else must die this death of eternal damnation, to

the extent that he has *community* with Jesus. Whoever is bound up
with Jesus *no longer dies alone, excluded from all community with God
and his future salvation*. . . . Whoever is bound up with Jesus dies,
to be sure, but *he dies in hope of the life of resurrection from the dead
that has already appeared in Jesus'* (my italics).

In other words, it would be wrong for us to think of ourselves
as sharing in Christ's risen life, which is the Holy Spirit, in the
same way that the members of the mystery cults believed that
they shared in the glory of their own resurrected gods. The Spirit
is not a sacred fluence that emanates out of the body of the exalted
Lord and is poured into our hearts when we come to the sacraments. Instead, the Spirit of Jesus is a *relationship*, and not some
kind of radiation. It is, in fact, that relationship of love, or fellowship, or, as Pannenberg puts it, of *community* that knits us closely
to God and to our fellow human beings in a personal way. It is, to
be precise, our individual participation in the relationship of community that even now obtains between Christ and his Father, and
between Christ and the rest of the human race, and that demands
that we each forget our own self-centred concerns in order to live
more for others, knowing that, if we do, our efforts will never be
ended by death. In this sense the Spirit is within us, but as yet
incompletely, as grace. Yet the presence of this Spirit of community in our lives assures us that our relationship, in Jesus, towards God and our fellows, will ultimately reach its completion
in the state of glory where there shall be nothing to hinder full
community and fellowship.

Thus, in the jargon of the examination room, Paul 'compares
and contrasts' Jesus with the mystery gods. But where the clients
of the mysteries held their gods to have won them the perfect
freedom of the state of glory by undergoing humiliations *on their
behalf* and without their own further involvement, 'Paul con-
trasted his own theology of resurrection with that of the enthusiasts.
His theology, too, is one of freedom: but it is that of people who
are attached to Jesus, who are therefore distinguished by his cross,
are called with him to suffer under the pious and the ungodly,
under tyrants and institutions, are capable of brotherhood, and

live on the strength of the commandments. Thus far it remains directed towards earthly realities, instead of fleeing into heavenly realms. This freedom is an anticipation of what things are to be like in the coming world and everlasting life. We talk of its being characterised by blessedness, and so we accommodate ourselves to the ideas and longings of other religions. That need not be wrong, but it is admissible only with one proviso: for us, blessedness is bound up with the sovereignty of Jesus. It is to be perfected in the future world, but it has already dawned on earth. If the freedom of the Christian man and the Christian church is centred in love, the resurrection of the dead is anticipated, because in it there appears the sovereignty of Jesus, which is perfected in the overcoming of death' (Käsemann, *Jesus Means Freedom*).

There should be nothing magical or automatic, therefore, about salvation as understood by the Christian. A man's future is not to be assured merely by arcane knowledge and sacred rite, but by the way he helps transform this world after the resurrection pattern.

This becomes obvious when we realise, for instance, that, when Paul speaks of mystery, he is not, like the cults, talking about some tight and closely-guarded secret reserved to an élite, but about the revealing to all mankind, in Jesus of Nazareth, of God's plan for the future of the world. In this sense, mystery, as Louis Bouyer has so convincingly shown, has a perfectly respectable Old Testament ancestry.

Again, though he will preach the unfathomable truth that Jesus lives in terms of a man's getting up out of the grave as if rising from sleep, much as the mystery cults thought of the resurrection of their gods or the Pharisees about the general resurrection that was to come at the Last Times, yet it is clear that he and the other New Testament writers are talking in picture language only. But they are talking, nevertheless, of events that are historically verifiable.

They are talking, in the first place, about the death of Jesus, about an execution that really took place, and not of vague legends about the gods of nature dying in the wintertime. And they are talking, too, of the unshakeable certainty of his followers, based upon experiences they found both utterly convincing and yet beyond their powers otherwise to describe, that this crucified Jesus was genuinely alive – and not merely as a lingering memory, as some kind of ghost, or simply in his message and ideals. Rather, the Jesus they had walked with in Galilee was with them still, but in a new kind of way they could not fully understand. Simultaneously at one with his Father, he yet dwelt among them in his Spirit, and they recognised his presence in the love they bore each other, and especially at the breaking of bread.

Furthermore, though holy meals and baptisms were common to many mystery cults, they were also common to the Jews at this time, since they came, in fact, from a common source and had a common ancestry in the fertility rites. But whereas the 'sacraments' of witchcraft or the mysteries sought to absorb and make use of the power of their god or to share in his other-worldly glory merely by taking part in such ceremonies, Judaism saw in such observances signs of the Passover. The penitential baptism of John reminded them of their forefathers' plunge into the Red Sea, and inspired them to make a new start themselves and a greater effort at living as God's People; and the sacred meal, by reminding them that the Lord who had led them to a land of plenty was always true to his promises, invited them to choose him again as their God as their predecessors had done at the time of the Covenant.

These rites the Christians reinterpreted as pointing to the new Passover and Covenant brought about in the death and exaltation of Jesus. They saw in baptism and the eucharistic meal Christ's invitation to his followers to dedicate themselves afresh to his Father and to humanity by seeking to die, with him, to those things in their own lives that inhibited their love for God and the brethren. Only by taking up the cross in this way would they be enabled to experience something of the transfiguring fellowship in the Spirit of the Lord that the sacraments held out to them.

4. Jesus and the Wise Men

If Jesus Christ was not a mystery god, neither was he a Gnostic redeemer. It is perfectly true that the Gnostics spoke of a demi-god who had existed from all eternity, who had come down from heaven to set men free from the grip of the powers of evil and who, before going back to heaven himself, had whispered to his chosen followers the secret information that would enable them to follow after him. It is true, too, that they frequently saw themselves as forming one body with this redeemer, so that the humiliations he had to undergo before defeating the evil powers were suffered on their behalf.

Nevertheless, as Dorothee Sölle points out in *Christ the Representative* (London, 1967), though Paul in particular will use language familiar both to the mystery religions and to Gnosticism, and though 'from Gnostic mythology came the idea of a *redeemed Redeemer* who constitutes one "body" with those who belong to him and whose experiences, such as death and resurrection, also happen to those who belong to his "body"', yet she will also point out that 'none of these various and divergent images being adequate to express the saving event, they were adopted and then set aside. . . . They circle around the reality . . . from various angles, and without the concept ever becoming explicit. Yet implicitly they radicalise the concept by liberating it from the magical view of representation.'

In other words, the death of Jesus differs radically from the redeeming work of the Gnostic demi-god. 'God, who despite the satisfaction already made, is still not content with the representative, continues to count on us, continues to look to us, to wait for us. For him, our hope, which is fixed on him, is not detachable and already settled. God is *not* content with our representative. Our representative speaks *for* us, but we ourselves have to learn to believe. . . . God allows us this freedom so that we should no longer be the prey of mythical preconceptions and prejudices. The New Testament declares this freedom began in Christ: it is celebrated in the hymn to Christ in Philippians which the apostle derived from the traditions of the primitive Church. The cosmic powers – under, above and on the earth – have paid homage to Christ. It is all up with them as 'powers', as mythical, fateful forces, the moment they acknowledged Christ. They have lost the power to terrorise anyone.'

And again she says: 'The recognition of Christ resulted in the abdication of the powers. Once lords of the world, they no longer have any say. When a man is still imprisoned in mythical thinking, he feels himself hemmed in by the world. He is caught in its toils, so it cannot become for him the medium of his self-realisation. At the mercy of irrational powers, he remains a child, underage, immature. But Christ, the man of God, reveals in his life what liberation from these powers, which still boast of their invincibility, could be like. He demythologises them. In mythical language, we express this by saying that he compels them to abdicate.'

Similarly, and to quote once again from Pannenberg's *Jesus, God and Man*, 'The representation of the Christ event as the descent and reascent of the Redeemer hardly involves a Gnosticising reinterpretation that misconstrued the Jewish tradition and that would be explained as a lack of understanding of the original meaning of the Christian message. Rather, the resurrected Lord's essential unity with God leads to the idea of pre-existence through its own intrinsic logic. This idea, whose emergence is understandable from the course of primitive Christian history of traditions itself, nevertheless came into contact with various currents in the atmosphere of the Hellenistic world. It was equally in the air for the Jewish anthropos doctrine, for the Jewish–Hellenistic Wisdom speculation, for the Hellenistic notion of outstanding men as appearances of a deity, and for the Oriental cults transformed into a doctrine of salvation for individuals as fostered in the mysteries. The unique persuasive power of the Christian concept of incarnation in the late classical world is explained by this situation. That the inner problematic of the Christ event pressed for an explication that simultaneously met the sense of truth and the desire for salvation *in its environment* reveals, not the weakness,

but the strength of the primitive Christian message and constitutes its missionary power' (my italics).

The first Christians, then, while quite prepared to speak about
Jesus in the kind of religious language current in their day, present
a saviour who is radically different from the minor deities of the
religions they encountered in their preaching. He was different,
too, as Pannenberg has reminded us, from the classical heroes who,
in learning to achieve complete peace of mind by remaining
supremely indifferent to all human suffering, including their own,
grew so much like the gods in their aloofness as to become
themselves divine.

Instead, Jesus revealed to us a God who cares for us in our pain.
He did so by himself plunging headlong into human suffering, in
order to change and transform it. He gave us the example of a
love that was ready to embrace death itself for the sake of the
beloved. And he showed us how such a love will take us beyond
all sorrow to the everlasting joy of perfect union with God and
with our brothers. 'It is utterly wide of the mark to interpret
Christ's suffering as stoicism,' says Sölle. In his earthly life, 'Christ
reserves nothing of himself to fall back on, to retreat into. He does
not even have "God behind him" to allow him to be indifferent
whether the world raged or rejoiced. Even for Christ, God was
the coming one still awaited. In the Christian view, suffering is
always the surrender of both self *and* God. Without this suffering,
which is rooted in dependence, representation is inconceivable –
except in a magical or substitutionary sense.'

5. Jesus and the Lords of the East

Neither the wise man of Aristotle nor of Plato, who learns to free
himself from matter by the gradual detachment of heart and mind
so as to leave himself free for the pursuit of purely spiritual realities, the Jesus we read about in the New Testament is also in
fundamental opposition to the typical religions of the east, to
both the Lords Krishna and Buddha.

Whereas, in the west, the sky-father religion was translated
into dualist philosophies that saw man's condition as that of a

spirit trapped in matter and his task as somehow to spiritualise this condition by escaping the insistent claims of the material world, in the east the work of translation produced a monism that saw matter as the inadequate manifestation of the spiritual reality, the one bright flame, that burned behind the universe and was the soul of man. In this view, man's task was to see beyond the apparent stability – and indeed desirability – of material things, since these were illusory and a snare set to prevent his soul's journey back to full union with and absorption into the one great spiritual reality.

Christ, on the other hand, leads his followers not away from but into the very heart of matter. He is the saviour not only of men but of the world in which men live. And, as such, he shows them that the approach to God is only to be made by giving oneself to this world of men and matter in a spirit of self-sacrificing love, so as to help it become more real as it moves on towards a future that has already been revealed in the rising of Jesus from the dead, not as soul or spirit or shade but as the full and complete human being his disciples knew in Galilee. If the religions of the world are typically escapist, other-worldly or magical, then Christianity can truly be claimed an anti-religion. Yet, as its history shows, it is an anti-religion that has been perpetually attracted, threatened and diverted by those very religious elements that Jesus shook off.

4

THE COUNTER-ATTACK

RELIGION WAS outlawed by the gospel of Christ. That is to say, in so far as religion can be typified as a neurotic response to the realities of our everyday human existence, and as the offer of an escape-route out of this world and its troubles by means of magical rites and secret truths, then Christianity has always rejected such a system. But that does not mean that the rejection has ever been completely successful. For religion is constantly fighting back; magic and false mysticism mount their counter-attack.

Adolf Exeler wrote in an article on *Education and Catechetics* that appeared in the March 1970 number of *Concilium*:

'The tendency to pursue religious knowledge and ritualism for their own sake is not exactly a new phenomenon in Christianity. It is as old as the faith itself, and must therefore be constantly exposed and resisted. We find that prophets fought it when, for instance, they turned against a ritualistic penitential system which encouraged people to hope that they could be reconciled with God through religious practices instead of genuine conversion. We find it also in Jesus' conflict with some groups among his contemporaries that put external religious practice above an authentic inner life.

'The unmasking of this diminution of religious life will always remain one of the tasks of ecclesiastical renewal. These features are the most subtle obstacle to religious life because this busying oneself about religion can easily cover up the real failures in life, and because those who want to purge this religious practice are often accused of being enemies . . . of the faith. *We should not*

*forget that Jesus was put to death by very pious people in the name of
God and for the sake of religion.'*

The counter-attack of religion, that is to say, can be seen most
clearly in the cross of Christ. And anyone who, following Jesus,
preaches the gospel likewise faces crucifixion.

For the gospel is subversive. It is revolutionary. It undermines
set patterns of thought and established ways of life. It tears from
our grasp the comforting playthings that religion affords and
throws down before us a discomforting challenge. No longer may
we seek security in our knowledge of the right formulae or our
involvement in the correct rituals. Instead, we have to try to live
up to the ideal that is presented to us in the deeds of Jesus of
Nazareth. If we would share in his destiny, if we would find our
salvation, then we must be prepared to turn our own lives and
standards and those of the world completely upside down for the
sake of brotherhood. We must learn to live for others, as he has
done, if we would find favour in his Father's eyes.

And though Paul could appeal to his converts to abandon their
pagan ways and undergo the 'spiritual revolution' demanded by
Christ, he still has to remind the Colossians that, just as Jesus has
done away with the Jewish law, 'so he got rid of the Sovereignties
and the Powers, and paraded them in public, behind him in his
triumphal procession'. For the fear of devils and the belief in
demi-gods still had its hold upon them. 'From now on,' Paul
goes on to warn them, 'never let anyone else decide what you
should eat or drink, or whether you are to observe annual
festivals, New Moons or sabbaths. These were only pale reflec-
tions of what was coming: the reality is Christ. Do not be taken
in by people who like grovelling to angels and worshipping
them; people like that are always going on about some vision they
have had, inflating themselves to a false importance with their
worldly outlook' (Col. 2:15-18).

Käsemann explains the situation of these early Christians about
whom Paul was so concerned. 'The young community of
Gentile Christians . . . had previously regarded the universe as
being governed by the stars, and they were convinced, like other

people in the same milieu, that human beings were constantly waylaid by demons. These Christians came mainly from the circles most subjected to the arbitrariness of the mighty and to the uncertain course of everyday events; and many of them therefore had joined the mystery religions, so as to be freed from the bonds of fate and from earthly fear. For them, Christ, by virtue of his resurrection, whose glory one shared through baptism, was the new mystery god. By humbling himself he had had pity on the lowly, and now, exalted at the right hand of the Father, he had broken through the power of the demons and stars. As Lord of all things, having conquered death and the devil, he had rendered them innocuous to those who were consecrated to him. Anyone who belonged to his expanding empire of peace had freedom now and ever' (*Jesus Means Freedom*).

But if the Church of the New Testament had to fight against this attempt to turn Jesus Christ into another mystery deity, it had also to do battle with Gnosticism.

As R. M. Grant and D. N. Freedman write, in *The Secret Sayings of Jesus*, 'The earliest Christianity, arising as it did out of Judaism, held firmly to the belief that God had acted in the past, was acting in the present, and would continue to act in the future. Some Christians, like some Jews, devised over-precise timetables for God's future action, and when the coming of the end of the world was delayed, they took refuge in dualistic spirituality. Losing the Christian faith in the return of Christ or the Jewish faith in the coming of God's Anointed, they looked only for the escape of the divine spark or true self from the evil world of matter and sin. At this point they became vulnerable to speculations derived from Greek philosophy or Oriental religions. They became vulnerable to Gnosticism. They became Gnostics.'

It was in recognition of this danger that Christ might so easily become demoted to the level of a mythical mystery-god or Gnostic demi urge that the early Church was so intolerant of any attempt at explaining the import of Jesus that failed to state clearly enough that he was at once a complete human being and yet, at the same time, the full and genuine communication of the

Godhead to us. He was neither the god-disguised-as-a-man of the Docetes, nor the man-who-became-divine of the Adoptionists, nor the non-divine superman of the Arians.

Yet, if we look at the Church of the fourth century, we find it characterised by three features that will nevertheless continue to threaten Christianity with a return to *mystery*, *false mysticism* and *magic*. These features are: *anti-Arianism*, *Platonism* and *establishment*.

1. Anti-Arianism and the Mysteries

In stressing the divinity of Christ against what was seen as an attempt to reduce Jesus to the level of the kind of demi-god worshipped in the mysteries, the orthodox began more and more to forget, not only that he was also truly a human being like ourselves and knew, during his earthly life, what it was to suffer the limitations of our everyday existence, but also that this fact of his human-ness is the first thing we can know and ought to say about him. For it is precisely because he is a real man that he can represent and redeem and mediate for men before the Father.

If Christ was divine, then he was to be feared as judge of all mankind. In particular, his coming among his people in the eucharist, seen as the advent of one far more terrifying than any mystery-deity, was an event to be dreaded and screened from sight. Let the wonder happen in a place set apart and specially consecrated, a sanctuary to be served by carefully-prepared ministers.

This tendency to re-create a holy place wherein a sacred caste might, by means of mysterious and hidden ceremonies, make mystically present the Lord of glory so that the laity might thus be sanctified has been a constant danger for Christianity, and particularly at any time of liturgical revival.

It was present at the time of the Cluniac reform with its notion that it was the duty of monks to celebrate the mysteries and sing the divine service on behalf of the lay-folk, who in turn ought to support this work with their alms and endowments. And it is present in the renewal of liturgy we are seeing in our own day.

One has only to look back to Dom Odo Casel and his efforts at the restoration of Christian worship in the 1940s to see that this is so. Reacting against the impoverished view of liturgy in the Catholic Church that saw it merely as a means for applying to the individual soul some of the fruits of grace that Jesus merited by his death on the cross long ago, Dom Odo asserted his theory of 'the presence of the mystery', a view he claimed to have found in the writings of St Paul and many of the early Church fathers.

In common with a growing number of theologians at the time, he rightly reminded us that it is not merely the death of Jesus, but his resurrection from the dead as Lord and Christ, that saves us, and that the life of the Christian on this earth is in some sense a continual participation in his saviour's dying to evil and rising to new life. Furthermore, it is this paschal mystery that, without being historically repeated, is yet present among us under signs whenever we take part in the liturgy of the Church.

Such a view runs a double risk. The first, which Casel carefully avoided but to which other Christians, particularly in Germany, succumbed, is the tendency to discount the cross as something over and done and as merely the means for Christ's rising, and to speak solely of the presence of the resurrected Lord and of our sharing, through the liturgy, in his heavenly glory alone. To quote from Käsemann once more: 'People who, like the Corinthian enthusiasts, are never tired of stressing the present power of the resurrection, at once resort to subtleties when the question of one's involvement in the cross is raised. . . . We must not fall into the error of the enthusiasts, who, for the sake of the risen Lord's presence, turn the cross into a historical affair. That must not be done, even if it is described as a unique supreme sacrifice, and a once-for-all reconciliation. Jesus' cross has not passed away on earth; it is now borne, not by him, but by us his delegates. . . . What ultimately matters is not that we genuinely believe and defend his preaching, but that we accept it as a call to walk as Jesus' disciples and to share in his death' (*Jesus Means Freedom*).

On the other hand, to speak of the presence of Christ in his passover too much in terms of the mystery religions and as though that presence were confined within the walls of our churches and during the performance of our rites is, as Louis Bouyer pointed out, to confuse the nature and purpose of that presence. For Jesus offers himself to us in personal encounter under the liturgical signs, not so as to take us out of this world and into glory here and now, but so that we might recognise his more important presence *in people*.

In liturgical worship, that is to say, we celebrate and seek to intensify a meeting with Jesus that takes place whenever we show love towards another human being. Furthermore, the Christ who is thus present in the liturgy and in our world is always the paschal Christ. Thus, to encounter Jesus in this personal and responsive way is to involve oneself inevitably in his death and resurrection, but not in any magical or mythical sense. It is to open one's heart anew to him and to his demands. It is to die a little more to one's own selfishness and to live a little more for others, by the love of the Holy Spirit which is his risen life. It is to prepare for one's own death, but as an event already undergone by Christ and changed by him into a way to new life. Again we must remember that the life Christ shares with us is precisely this relationship of love that he bears towards his Father and towards every member of the human race, a relationship in which we can participate only to the extent that we are dead to a wrong-headed love of self.

It is certainly possible, however, to interpret Casel and even the Liturgy Constitution of Vatican II in such a way as to imagine that the only real contact we make with Jesus in his rising from the dead is in church and during the liturgical rites. It is also possible, from the same sources, to see the Church's year as making especially present to us, at the various sacred seasons, particular aspects of the mystery of Jesus' passover. Thus Casel implies that the *paschal vigil* is the holiest time of the year, since it is then that the death and resurrection of Christ are most powerfully present and available to his people.

Yet, in fact, the purpose of trying to remember or fix our attention upon certain aspects of the life of Christ in our round of liturgical worship is not to try to return to or re-create the event remembered in some kind of 'sacred time' that is nevertheless non-historical. Instead, it is so that the liturgical encounter with the Lord might be more effective for each of us personally in that the particular celebration is meant to help us revive our openness and love in a particular way that will correspond to the event thus remembered.

For we cannot stress too much that the Christ we meet in men and in the sacraments is a Christ who always requests our complete death to self and offers us in return the fullness of love. While there cannot, consequently, be degrees of the presence of the paschal Christ in that Jesus always offers himself to us completely, no matter how ineffectually we meet him in our limited response, yet the purpose of his presence in the liturgy and throughout its annual cycle is always so that we might recognise and respond to him more intensely when we meet him in our fellow human beings. Without this caution, we run the danger of sheer ritualism and of seeing the due and decent performance of the liturgy as our main aim in life, the end and not the means to full and conscious Christian living.

Käsemann, it seems to me, sums up the effects of this temptation admirably.

'The Christian church . . . has always had something of the mystery cult about it. This began when the church entered the Hellenistic world, in which the redemptive call could be heard only as it was sounded by the dominant mystery religions. . . . We ought to recognise and concede the pagan antecedents of all these sacred matters: Jesus the cultic God, the holy year as the backbone of the calendar and of life, the priestly office which makes the rest of God's people the laity, the holy place which is to be approached with pious awe and is separated by thick walls from the world, the ceremony which brings us into the company of the angels and saints. . . . We have to see before us him who, walked the country roads of Galilee and Samaria to Jerusalem with no home of his own and associating with everyone, if we are to appreciate the far-reaching contrast between the beginnings and the present day. *If he had wanted to have this present-day situation, he could have founded a sanctuary such as the Qumram community in the desert and sent his missionaries out from there. In that case the cross itself would hardly have been needed; neither Jews nor Romans nor Greeks had any objection to a new cult'* (*Jesus Means Freedom*, my italics).

2. Platonism and Mystical Flight

The Hellenistic background of the early Christians plus their realisation that the return of Jesus was farther off than once had been supposed led them increasingly to look upon Jesus as revealing the *divine order* that rules the universe and seeks to govern the lives of men. He was *epiphany* more than *eschaton*, and made manifest, in his earthly existence, the spiritual reality that underlies the human condition here and now, though largely hidden from view by the veils of matter, rather than proclaiming, by his rising from the dead, the future of the whole creation.

Thus Christianity inherited, via the Platonic idealism that, according to Karl Rahner, has bedevilled the Church for almost two thousand years, that distrust of matter as obscuring the brightness of the divine glory and holding back the soul of man from its fullness of encounter with the ultimate spiritual reality that has its roots not in the gospel but in the old creation myths.

Such an attitude was bound to focus the attention of Christians more and more upon the saving value of the incarnation and thus in time to give rise to feasts of Christmas or Epiphany. The resurrection, in consequence, came to be looked upon as the full revelation of a glory that had belonged, in fact, to Jesus from the first moment of his existence, while the cross was explained as his way both of impressing upon us the horror with which God views our violations of the divine order, and also of paying off our debt to win us back from the devil's grip and of taking on our punishment to appease the Father's just wrath. Thus began that concentration on the cross and neglect of the resurrection that, as we have seen, predominated in western Christianity until quite modern times.

But if Christ reveals the divine order, it is so that his followers might observe and realise that order in their own lives. Thus the kingdom of God will only arrive in its completeness when individual Christians have learned to fulfil perfectly the law that governs human nature in general and their own state of life in particular. So the path is prepared for the high medieval concept of Christendom as the kingdom of God on earth and the reflection of the heavenly kingdom to which the soul will take flight at death if it has done its duty sufficiently well while in this world.

Again, if Christ reveals spiritual realities and teaches us to save our souls by shunning the distractions of the earthly city and seeking our escape from the coils of matter, then spiritual interests and the spiritual society that protects and promotes them will rightly seek to dominate the secular world. Hence the claims of Church over state that were so triumphantly expressed by Hildebrand and that continued to be made until well into the present century (and, indeed, were only officially disavowed by the Roman Church in Vatican II's unequivocal statement that the Church is *servant* of the world).

Hence, too, the growth of a view of the Church's role as arbiter of morals and interpreter of the natural law that made either Pope, for example, or Bible into the oracle of God. Rather than looking upon Christ's ethical teaching as a challenge to abandon Stoical moderation or the *golden mean* of Aristotle and to live, instead, more according to the model and ideal presented by the life and death of Jesus of Nazareth, Christians began to see it as a secret code that they alone could decipher. At its crudest, this attitude is revealed today in, for instance, the Jehovah's Witness who rummages through the Apocalypse to seek out hidden directives or the Roman Catholic who believes the Pope has only to pray hard enough for the divine answer to any of the moral problems besetting mankind to be relayed to him from on high.

Like the meditation of Plato's wise man that pierces through the material universe to make contact with a spiritual realm of ideas that is but palely reflected in the world of matter, so there is a strong current persisting in Christianity that has always interpreted prayer as the soul's transcending its earthly and temporary

C

dwelling in order to find a fuller union with the supreme, eternal and spiritual being who is God.

We find such an attitude in the strain of medieval mysticism that was influenced by neo-Platonism and particularly by the writings then attributed to Denis the Areopagite. We find it even more starkly expressed in the *devotio moderna* of the early renaissance, that spiritual movement originating in the low countries that took for its handbook the *Imitation of Christ*, where again and again the human body is described as the soul's prison-house, the material universe as its snare and distraction, and death as its final release.

In the counter-reformation, this Platonic tendency still endured in the attitude, discernible in the works of Theresa of Avila and John of the Cross, that the activity of prayer is far superior to that of the loving service of others in the world. For prayer unites the soul directly with its Maker, while good works merely meet him indirectly through his creatures.

Those who are called to the life of prayer are therefore highly favoured. They belong to an élite, since they are invited to a kind of union with God more real and genuine than that which the general run of Christians is able to experience. It is this kind of thinking that underlies the idea, still so dear to many, that the so-called *Religious life* is superior to that of the laity, and this despite Vatican II's clear implication, when it described the communal life in vows as but one way of living out the vocation given to every Christian at baptism, that this grading of the People of God into first- and second-class citizens is no longer tenable. It lies, too, behind the idea that, for a Religious, periods of prayer, the novitiate and the annual retreat are the really holy times in his or her life. For it is then that one withdraws as fully as may be from the distractions of 'the world' and from one's *horizontal* relationship with others in order to pursue the far more important *vertical* relationship with the Almighty.

Whatever we are to say now about prayer – and it is a subject that will be discussed in a later chapter – we may not, I think, give it this Platonic slant. In fact, we meet God most fully and really, on the level of ontological encounter and union in the Spirit, whenever we meet our fellow human beings in love. However intensely we may become aware of the full import of such a meeting by reflecting upon it, and thus prepare ourselves to meet God, in Christ, more generously when in future we move among men, this prayerful meditation can never replace our actual loving of other people, for which there is no substitute at all of saving worth. On the contrary, our service of others is the *fruit* of prayer rather than a distraction from it, since both activities, when correctly undertaken as double requirements in the life of any Christian, are in fact horizontal *and* vertical at the same time, uniting us in loving fellowship with God only to the extent that they unite us in loving fellowship with our neighbour.

Christian mysticism, therefore, while using techniques and knowing psychological experiences that are similar if not identical to those undergone in Hinduism, Moslem Sufism and western occultism, explains them very differently. It sees them, not as ways of leaving behind this unreal world of matter nor as guarantees of union with the divine, but as productive of a kind of God-consciousness that will remind us most intensely of what we are about in a world that, through us, the Lord wishes to transform. And the only test it offers by which we may gauge the depth of our union with a God of whose glory we are trying to become more aware is the extent to which, in fact, we really do love our neighbour. Unless our mysticism helps us do just that, then it is leading us away from and not into union with the ultimate reality.

And, in fact, it is often the case that those who would explain their practice of meditation in terms of a Hindu-type mystical flight are nevertheless distinguished by a deep concern for the troubles of their brethren on this earth that can easily put the Christian to shame. But, whereas a Mahatma Ghandi or a John Lennon would see their work for love and peace as a way of helping other human beings escape from the bonds of *maya* or material illusion, the Christian would see the same endeavours as in reality helping in the redeeming of men and matter from their common slavery to corruption by leading them on towards their common destiny in glory.

3. The Establishment and Magic

Though the first Christians shrank from applying pagan titles to the ministers of the gospel and reserved the name of priest exclusively but metaphorically to Jesus Christ in his work of worshipping the Father and to the baptised Christian who shared explicitly in that worship, gradually the elders (presbyters) and overseers (bishops) began to be likened to the priests and high priests of the Old Testament and, particularly with the establishment of Christianity as an official religion of Constantine's empire in 313, to the priesthoods of paganism. Now that the old religion was on the decline and there seemed little danger of confusing it with Christianity, so the Christian leaders felt free not only to take over the roles in society but also the very names of, for example, the pagan supreme pontiff of Rome and his cardinals.

The same is true of the Church's adoption of terms like temple, altar and sacrifice. The eucharist, originally a meal celebrated by the Christian community in which the members gave themselves anew, in the self-offering Christ, to the Father by giving themselves more whole-heartedly to one another, came increasingly to be seen as a rite performed by a sacred caste called the clergy in a holy spot set apart to appease an angry deity on behalf of a people not qualified themselves to celebrate the *sacred mysteries*.

This leaning towards religion in worship was reinforced with the conversion of northern Europe and particularly of the Germanic tribes. Frantically afraid of the devils that inhabited rocks and stones and trees; trusting in their long-dead heroes, whom they had elevated into tribal gods; and seeking the sacred fluence that holy objects and actions and spells could draw down from the heavens; the northern peoples were, in short, only too ready, after their conversion, to convert Christianity, in their turn, into the magical system they so desired.

In the churches that had been built on their old holy places, they would beg for aid at the bones of the particular bishop or missionary who had first preached the gospel to their fathers, and that with such fervour that they had somehow to be reminded that Jesus was (in an anti-Arian oversimplification) their one and only God, and that the reserved sacrament was on that account far more efficacious than the relics of any saint. Thus, in the Germanies, the bread of the eucharist began to be placed in silver or crystal containers and carried into battle or round the fields so as to prosper the works of the tribe.

Blessings they saw less as prayers for the divine favour than as spells by which power came forth from the hand or mouth of the priest to drive away demons from whatever he so blessed. Incense, holy water and signs of the cross were also held to have magical powers. Thus the priest would make the wonder-working sign to drive the devils out and create a holy place before setting host or chalice down upon the altar. He would then ring them round three times with incense smoke, so creating a sacred circle no demon dare violate, whether he came from above, from the earth or from the underworld. So the blessings and exorcisms, used so sparingly in the old Roman rite, began to be multiplied and performed in triplicate in response to tendencies that were blatantly magical.

Against such a background, the medievals were obviously encouraged to interpret the Christian sacraments and gospel ministry in a magical way. The character of the priest, instead of being seen as the visible expression, when he preached the word and presided over the eucharist, of his call to serve the community in a particular way, began to be understood by many as a mysterious 'mark or seal on the soul' that gave him the awesome 'power' of 'confecting' the sacraments, and in particular of changing bread and wine into the body and blood of Christ.

A misunderstanding of the doctrine that the sacraments achieve their effects *ex opere operato* added to this tendency. Originally, this simply meant that, no matter how unworthy the minister, the sacraments he celebrates still represent a genuine offer of grace made by Christ to his faithful. However, it added, this offer is only effective to the extent that it is accepted, and it is only accepted to the extent that the recipient places no obstacle of sin or selfishness in the way.

However, this doctrine was taken popularly to mean that the sacraments worked automatically. Whether their celebration aroused faith and love in the recipient and helped him remove any obstacles to grace became unimportant. What mattered was that the right words were spoken, the correct gestures made, the proper materials used. Once that were done, then the faithful would be irradiated with grace in spite of themselves, so it seemed.

Geoffrey Diekmann reminds us of this attitude with regard to the mass in an article he wrote in an American magazine, *The Priest* (1969):

'How many of you can recall retreats in which the retreat master reminded the priests before him that they have been ordained to take the place of Christ, and therefore in no way may their personal preferences or personality intrude upon the sacred action? It is Christ who acts *ex opere operato*, and therefore the celebrant of the mass should, as it were, be a *faceless priest*, anonymous. How far have we come from those ancient days. . . . Emphasis on the sanctification of man means precisely that it is up to the priest to make the mass such an experience that it really does stir the faith, and does stir, above all, charity. This is our ministerial task and it is a huge task, for it does not take place automatically!'

The magical attitude Diekmann complains of is to be found explicitly stated in *The Christ, Psychotherapy and Magic* by the Anglo-Catholic priest A. D. Duncan (London, 1969).

Describing how a well-known magician sees his robes as de-personalising him and as helping his magic since they are charged with 'a certain etheric energy', Duncan goes on to comment: 'The instincts recorded here are not confined altogether to the occult lodges; the eucharistic vestments have a similar function of covering the personality of the priest and suggesting Christ, whose *clothes* they are, being stylised replicas of the clothing of the eastern Roman empire of the first century. . . . Although Christians do not speak of the eucharistic vestments being *charged*, they are nevertheless blessed – set apart for this specific purpose. The ceremonial of the eucharist, the externals, is in a perfectly valid sense *magical*.'

Indeed, Duncan seems to delight in treating of the mass as a superior and more powerful kind of magic, and quotes with approval the opinion of another magician, Dion Fortune, (who can also boast that 'we work the mass with power') when she says: 'I am not a Catholic, and never shall be, because I would not submit to their discipline, nor do I believe that there is only One Name under heaven whereby men may be saved, much as I respect that Name, but *I know power when I see it*, and I respect it' (*The Mystical Qabalah*, my italics).

Miss Fortune has seen in the mass something she shouldn't. Far from being a work of power, the eucharist is a celebration of the Christian community in which, as their servant and in their name, the priest gives thanks over bread and wine as together they remember the redeeming work of Christ. In so doing, he proclaims the true meaning and identity that Jesus gives to this food and drink. It is not a question, therefore, of the community having power over Christ and drawing him down upon the altar, but of the Lord inviting his faithful to take and eat and in so doing to reunite themselves with God and one another in the love that is his Spirit-life.

Again, although in the prayer of thanksgiving the bread and wine become the new reality that is the risen Lord, yet the attempt to isolate the exact moment when the change takes place, as though it were something chemical, is not only fruitless but also misleading.

It implies, first of all, that the change is merely a matter of saying the right words, and that, even apart from or outside of a eucharistic celebration, the priest has only to whisper the correct formula, utter the magic spell, for bread or wine to become Christ. Secondly, it suggests that the change is material, not spiritual, and that the Lord is in consequence present in such a way, underneath the appearances of bread and wine, that he can be physically touched or even hurt – in short, as though he were present in space and time, as we can be present to one another.

Such an idea lay behind the medieval cult of the *black mass*; it also underlay the explanations of the sacrifice of the mass, current before Trent, that saw Christ as slain anew by the words of the priest or talked with wonder of hosts dripping blood; and it lies behind the superstition, still all too commonly taught in Catholic schools, that to touch the host with one's teeth is a mortal sin!

Magic above all, it seems to me, enters into the mass when we in our day misunderstand the sacrificial aspect of the eucharist. For the mass is a sacrifice precisely because it is a meal – a meal in which, in union with the self-offering Lord, we give ourselves to his Father and ours by giving ourselves to the service of others. Our memorial of Calvary in no way 'slays Christ anew', either really or mystically, but rather puts us into contact with the Christ who is for ever in the attitude of one who *was* slain – that is, in the attitude of complete and loving self-surrender.

As Robert Ledogar reminds us in an article, *Table Prayers and Eucharist*, that appeared in the February 1970 number of *Concilium*:

'The problem . . . is one that theologians struggled with a generation ago when trying to explain how the mass is a *sacrifice*. They went to Comparative Religion to look for definitions of sacrifice only to find that (1) the experts did not agree; (2) Christianity claims to have transcended the very conceptions on which any such definitions would rest. Marrett develops his distinction between a sacramental meal and a festal meal on the basis of taboo and *holy fear*. The Christian theologian must insist that Jesus came to destroy all that. The many gospel scenes, especially the eating scenes after the resurrection in Luke and John, have about them a familiarity and a naturalness which seem so opposed to the fear-dominated religion of so-called primitive societies.'

It should be clear by now that magic enters into our attitude towards the eucharist and the other sacraments when we begin to look upon them as *objects* (including objective rites) that automatically give *power*, rather than *events* in which Christ invites us to recognise and celebrate our new *relationship* with God the Father and with the human community by loving both as he does, that is, in his Spirit. Furthermore, sacramentals, blessings and the like are meant to increase this relationship (that is grace at work in our lives) and not to impart some kind of sacred fluence.

For magic threatens, and especially in the Roman Catholic Church, since, despite the care with which theologians may justify, in a rational and non-magical way, Catholic practices approved of by ecclesiastical authority, yet many of these are in fact regarded superstitiously by the ordinary faithful.

We do not believe God can be placated and grace won automatically: yet the practice of the mass stipend often implies as much. We have no holy objects or lucky charms that guarantee God's favour or protection: yet medals, scapulars, statues and pictures are too often claimed to do just that. We know of no sacred numbers that irresistibly impress the Almighty and wheedle from him what we want: yet this is exactly how many simple folk think of devotions like the Nine First Fridays and certain noveneas and repeated prayers with astounding promises attached. We recognise no holy place: yet Jesus is popularly thought to be *locally* present *in* the tabernacle which is *in* the church building, and the eucharist often seen as manifesting the only real presence that there is of the Lord on this earth, and not as his invitation to us to come and eat this sacred food with love so that, by its means, he might increase his loving presence in our hearts; or places like the Holy Land, Rome or Lourdes, instead of being looked upon as poignant reminders able to open our hearts up to Christ more completely, are often treated in a pagan way as though the actual terrain were somehow closer to heaven and impregnated with divine power and the 'genius of the place'. We know of no sacred caste, since all the baptised share in the priesthood of Christ and are equally obliged, each in his own sphere, to offer their lives with him to the Father in worship: yet priests and religious, by their dress and life-style, often find themselves treated as people with power or extra holiness, a race set apart and the only true Christians.

Have we not need enough, then, to affirm, by our ridding the Church of all that might lead to such superstitious misunderstandings of the plain meaning of the gospel, that Christianity cannot tolerate magic, and that the counter-attack of religion has signally failed? At present, the opposite seems all too often true!

5

THE ROCK OF SECURITY

RELIGION LOOKS for security. Its natural tendency is therefore to search out ways in which it may control the whims of fortune by harnessing the power of its gods to do good or to harm. Thus it not only concocts magical rites by which it claims to channel such power to the advantage of its own adherents but it also frequently sets great store by oracles who will utter sacred words that, once deciphered, will provide the key to understanding the secrets of the future and how the gods may best be served and their dooms best avoided. This oracular 'uttering' may come from the lips of some chosen individual; often it emerges from the pages of a sacred book.

Christianity offers no such security. It has no book or personage who may pretend to predict times and seasons or provide mankind with a superbly reliable horoscope. Its concept of revelation is, however, far more fundamentally reassuring.

The relationship of love that all men may have with God to the extent that they enter into fellowship one with another is a relationship that human beings have long sought to understand. That is to say, men have, to some degree, been able to see a deity revealing himself from within their communal relationships, a God who *is* love. But the Word or self-disclosure of God, coming to men in the love and understanding that is the Holy Spirit at work in their lives, reached its fullest expression in Jesus, who is that self-disclosure become fully human.

But Jesus the man *was* the Word because he was also the *recipient* of that Word, and that so completely as to be and to communicate that Word. Thus Jesus always received the Word as fully as possibly in his human heart and consciousness – that is to say, with love and understanding. And this Word of God that proclaimed to him that he was the beloved Son of the Father was also a Word that saved, since it rescued him from the drawbacks of being an earthbound member of a fallen race and from the fate of death itself.

The risen Christ is the full Word of God to us. He is the Word who displays a Father who can likewise save us all from death, a God who is, in Karl Rahner's phrase, 'the absolute future of the human race'. For in Jesus we see our future laid bare.

Following Gabriel Moran's explanation, we may say that we who believe and who accept Jesus as Word of the Father do so by entering into his own human consciousness of God. That is to say, we share in Christ's understanding of the Father when we consciously accredit him as revealing such a God to us. Furthermore, this revelation tells us that the loving and self-offering relationships that all good men and women seek to create with others are in fact so many instances of participation in the love of Christ, the Spirit that, in uniting them to their fellows, also unites them, without their necessarily being aware of it, to God their heavenly Father.

The Christian community that understands and recognises this presence of the saving Spirit of the risen Lord in our world accepts Jesus explicitly on behalf of the wider human community. Revelation therefore consists, in the first place, of Jesus' own conscious acceptance of the saving Word of God, and then of the Church's conscious acceptance of Jesus as that Word in whom the Father's salvation is brought to men. In this sense, therefore, revelation takes place throughout history and whenever a human being's understanding of this Word of God either dawns or deepens.

And this revelation who is Christ brings not comfort but a challenge. Far from having delivered to the Church a set of truths, an exhaustive list of doctrinal propositions couched in language so refined that it need never be changed, he has rather committed it to the struggle of trying to discern more clearly and express more satisfactorily the depths of meaning to be found in his life, death and exaltation. At the same time, without disclosing the forthcoming history of the human race in reassuring detail, he has nevertheless proclaimed himself to be the future of that race (whatever that may mean) and resurrection to be its goal. Yet this is a future men can only bring about by the unremitting effort at trying to live for others as he has done. And Jesus nowhere promises that this task will be rewarded with earthly comfort or crowned with worldly success. On the contrary, he guarantees only difficulties, persecution and the cross in this life to those who would follow his way.

A Christian is therefore lulling himself into a false sense of security if he thinks it sufficient for salvation that he believe the correct doctrines, or imagines indeed that his own particular communion is already so possessed of the truth that it has no further need of seeking a deeper and more comprehensive understanding of the gospel. It is a species of gnosticism to assume that knowledge alone can win redemption, and of Hellenistic idealism to imply that orthodoxy is more important than charity.

However, if the desire for an oracle is frankly non-Christian, it is nevertheless a desire to which Christians have often given way. We need only look at the attitudes of different bodies of Christians in the past (and even today) towards, for example, *inspiration and the Bible* or *infallibility and the pope*.

The assertion that the Bible was inspired and free from error generally meant, until modern times, that it was put on a par with the sacred scriptures of the religions, since it was widely assumed that it therefore contained no mistakes of any kind and was accurate in its every statement, whether of geography, history or biology, since each word had been miraculously dictated by God by the power of his Spirit.

But, as William Neil puts it (*The Truth About the Early Church*, 1970), 'The literal infallibility of the scriptures was a sufficient formula to stifle all intelligent enquiry. Now that this panacea has been found wanting, what are we left with? I believe myself that we are left with something far better, something which affirms what is the essential character of the whole Bible, namely that it is the Word of God conveyed to man by human hands.'

For the scriptures are the product of a community searching to understand its God more adequately and putting down the results of its enquiries in the kind of language and ideas that were current at the time of writing and in its own milieu. The inspiration of the Spirit should not, therefore, be looked upon as some magical fluence possessing the biblical author like a divine hypnosis. Instead, it is at work within the communal effort at understanding, so that the written witness to that community's faith will, in a thoroughly fallible and human fashion, nevertheless testify accurately to the Word of God *to the extent that it has been heard by the community*.

Neil, in the book we have just mentioned, quotes J. D. Smart as saying, in this regard, 'It is just because the prophets and apostles are so indwelt by the Spirit of God that they are so robustly, freely, independently and concretely human. The incoming of God's Spirit does not eliminate their human qualities so that they become mere puppets of God, but in the fullest sense it makes them *men* of God' (*The Interpretation of Scripture*, 1961).

Thus the Christian Church, in a perfectly human way, has taken the written witness of the People of God of old as a faithful expression of their developing and inadequate Old Testament beliefs, and crowned it with the writings the same Church has selected, in all their variety and with their different authors, styles and outlooks, as expressing genuinely and adequately the faith of the new People of God.

Two questions arise here that the scholars are only beginning to face, and from which they have so far shielded the public. One is this. How far is Christianity exclusively the fulfilment of Judaism and therefore of its sacred writings? Does the fact that Christ was a Jew mean that he is not so completely the fulfilment of the pagan religions too, and of their own creeds and oracles and writings?

The second question is this. Most Christians would now admit that the doctrine of inspiration does not at all rule out the possibility and indeed the fact that the Bible contains error. So far,

however, we have tended to restrict its mistakes to the fields of
geography, history, physics and the like. Must we also go on to
hold that it is theologically inerrant, or may we not admit that
St Paul, for example, made and taught a blunder about the
proximity of Christ's second coming, or that his attitude to
women was theologically incorrect?

Young people, when they study scripture, will often ask why
we need to turn somersaults in order to prove that the New Testament writers were always correct in their statements about God.
While accepting the New Testament as the Church's written
witness, some of them tend to see this refusal to admit any theological error at all in the sacred writings as evidence of a magical
outlook.

On the other hand, we find the young people who are joining
the fundamentalist Jesus movement in the United States treating
the Bible very much as an oracle, and claiming that other books
beyond the scriptures and other kinds of learning beyond knowledge of the scriptures are quite unnecessary. The Bible contains
all truth, whether religious, scientific or philosophical.

If, nevertheless, this oracular attitude to the Bible is generally
declining nowadays, the Roman Catholic doctrines of the infallibility of the pope and of the Church seem still exceedingly
prone to magical interpretations.

If we are to understand the infallibility of the pope as at all
meaningful, and if we are to free ourselves from any idea of his
being in constant touch with a deity who informs him at all
times as to what exactly is the truth in faith or morals, then we
must, I think, exchange the abstract and legal term 'infallibility'
with the concrete Hebrew image of 'rock'.

We are frequently told in the Old Testament that Yahweh is
the rock of Israel. And he is rock because his Word is utterly
reliable. His promise of a blessed future for his People holds good
for ever and is worthy of all their trust, no matter how hopeless
and unpromising things might at present appear.

At the same time, the rabbis in the days of Jesus also spoke of
another foundation-stone for Israel. They told the legend of how,

when Yahweh first decided to build up a People for himself, he
came down to earth and poked about in the desert with a long
stick, trying to find a firm and solid basis upon which the house
of Israel could be constructed. Everywhere he prodded, he found
nothing but sand – until his stick suddenly struck rock. *And the
rock was Abraham.*

It is not only the promising Word of God, therefore, that is the
rock upon which the Chosen People may rest secure, but also the
answering faith of Abraham in that Word. For, if anyone really
had confidence in the promises of Yahweh in the midst of what
looked like a desperate situation, it was he. The stories of his
answering God's call, of his leaving house and lands and kinsfolk
to become a desert wanderer, of the utter trust he put in the Word
of the Lord despite his own length of years, all combined to make
of the shadowy figure of the great patriarch a symbol and a by-
word among the Jews for fidelity.

And this was true even for Jewish Christians, like those in Rome
who were reminded by Paul of the faith of their great ancestor.

'Though it seemed Abraham's hope could not be fulfilled, he
hoped and he believed, and through doing so he did become the
father of many nations exactly as he had been promised: "Your
descendants will be as many as the stars." Even the thought that
his body was past fatherhood – he was about a hundred years old –
and Sarah too old to become a mother, did not shake his belief.
Since God had promised it, Abraham refused either to deny it or
even to doubt it, but drew strength from faith and gave glory to
God, convinced that God had power to do what he had promised.
This is the faith that was "considered as justifying him". Scripture,
however, does not refer only to him but to us as well when it
says that his faith was thus "considered"; our faith too will be
"considered" if we believe in him who raised Jesus our Lord
from the dead, Jesus who was put to death for our sins and raised
to life to justify us' (4:18–25).

The rock-like faith of Abraham upon the rock of God's
promise, his belief that, despite any appearances to the contrary,
Yahweh was still completely reliable in everything that he said,

this was Israel's foundation-stone in that, if the People of God was to grow firm and four-square and take up its inheritance, then it, too, must share in Abraham's faith. The Israelites must emulate the absolute trust of their founding-father that God would be true to his Word, no matter how daunting the circumstances of the moment.

But the one People was traditionally thought of as having been made up of twelve tribes, each with an ancestral patriarch of its own; and the twelve patriarchs were also held to be, with Abraham, the foundation-stones of the one nation.

Thus we have the Word of the Lord as the fundamental rock that upholds Israel, a promise that is always valid and will never fail; then Abraham as rock because of his believing fully in that Word; and finally the patriarchs, who share in the rock-like function of Abraham in that they, too, were men of faith whose trust in the Word their descendants must copy if they are to find their security in God.

If the Word of Yahweh, as heard by patriarchs and prophets, is the rock of the old Israel, so that Word made flesh in Jesus of Nazareth is the rock of the new. Jesus the Word is the cornerstone on which the Church is built, the one foundation for the reconstructed People of God. He is the stone the builders of the old house of Israel rejected and upon whom the faithless stumble and fall. He is the rock that is struck by the spear of death but that pours out, at resurrection, the water of life upon the world. He is the living keystone into which his followers are built, to become themselves living stones that share his spirit and form, with him, one temple devoted to the praise and worship of the Father (1 Peter 2:4–10).

Jesus is rock because he is the Word of God's promise. In his rising from the dead, he displays and holds out to all who believe in him what the destiny shall be both of themselves and of all the many non-believers of good will and conscience whom they represent. No matter how difficult and hopeless things might seem, nevertheless the risen Lord is present among men as the future God has ordained for them, and it is this enduring presence of the Word that the Church recognises and acknowledges. For it is the vocation of this new People of God to act on behalf of the wider community of mankind in accepting that Word in faith and trust as a Word who gives hope to the whole human race, a Word who is sure and true, a Word upon whom all men may rely, a Word who never leaves the Church or abandons humankind.

But Peter, too, is a rock. If the Church is the new Israel, then he is its Abraham. Such, according to Oscar Cullmann, is the central affirmation of the early Christians about the position of Simon, as the 'change-of-name' episode specially inserted into Matthew 16 bears powerful witness.

The Simon whom Matthew also presented as frequently lacking in faith during Jesus' earthly life, who has hardly enough trust to walk with his Lord on the water, who acts as God's enemy in advising his master to avoid his oncoming Passion and who, out of fear, ends by betraying him is also the Peter who is given charge over the new synagogue of Christians and carries the keys of God's household, who is to shepherd the new flock of the Lord, who is to strengthen the faith of his brethren and who, in the first part of Acts, is indisputably the central figure in the apostolic Church. For, according to the passage in Matthew we have been speaking of, he has been renamed by Jesus as Cephas, Petros, the Rock on which the Church is to be built (Matt. 16:18).

The incident is placed just before Jesus' first prediction of his death, or, in other words, when the promises made by God through him are to begin to look as though they have failed. It is here that Peter professes explicitly, 'You are the Christ, the Son of the living God.'

If Jesus the Word is the rock of the Church, then Peter is also its foundation-stone, but in a secondary sense, because of his absolute faith in that Word. But the new Abraham is not alone in this capacity. He is one of a company of twelve patriarchs, those who, Jesus said, would 'sit on twelve thrones to judge the twelve tribes of Israel' (Matt. 19:28). For, as Paul tells the Church in Ephesus, 'You are part of a building that has apostles and prophets for its foundations, and Christ Jesus himself for its main cornerstone. As every structure is aligned on him, all grow into one holy temple in the Lord; and you too, in him, are being built into a house where God lives, in the Spirit' (2:20–22).

But in what sense does the faith of the faithless Peter and of his weak and doubting brethren make them the foundation-stones of the Church? For doubting and uncertain they often were during their Lord's lifetime with them, and particularly so at his death. Their lack of trust is surely no example to us who follow after, just as Peter's isolated witness to Jesus as the Christ hardly makes up for his forthcoming threefold denial.

Instead, we should look at this affirmation of Peter's as a reading back into the days before the resurrection of the kind of faith he and his fellow-apostles were to show when once they had met with the risen Lord. For it is in this mysterious yet utterly convincing encounter with the Christ of glory that they become the bedrock on which the Church is to be reared.

As Paul writes to 'God's building', or the church, in Corinth, 'By the grace God gave me, I succeeded as an architect and laid the foundations' for their community. But what was this grace of Paul's? Fundamentally, it was his own meeting with the exalted Jesus whose followers he once had persecuted. For it was this that made of him, too, a 'witness of the resurrection' with a valid claim to being an apostle. And how did he go on to lay the foundations of the Church of Christ in Corinth and elsewhere? By his preaching; by telling others of what he had experienced; by proclaiming his belief that Christ was risen from the dead.

Thus it is by their preaching of the resurrection that the apostles create the Church. And those who believe what they are saying, the communities that spring into being by accepting their testimony, have come in their turn to share in the apostles' faith. For it is not words they have received, but *the* Word, Jesus Christ, to whom, with Peter and his brethren, they now consciously cling. Christ becomes their rock because he has been proclaimed to them by the rock-like witness of the apostles and has been acknowledged by them with something of the apostles' rock-like faith.

Such, then, is the main function of the founding-fathers of the new Israel. They announce the good news, they relay the living Word of God, they pronounce the promise that the risen Lord is with men and leading them on to perfect freedom. And this preaching role of theirs is essentially a *service*. No matter how vital, how necessary and important their function as messengers of Jesus, it is one that they perform, not to their own honour and glory, but as servants of the Word, for the good of mankind and the building-up of the Church. They are the men, after all, who must wash their brothers' and sisters' feet.

And this applies especially to Peter. As undoubted head or *primate* of the apostolic band or *college*, he above all must preach the gospel fearlessly and be prepared to be led off in bonds to execution like his master, so self-effacing must be his service, so confident his hope of resurrection.

The small Christian communities that arose in the towns and cities of the Roman Empire were themselves therefore in the *apostolic succession*, as indeed are all those who, because of the continuing testimony of the Church of the apostles, will also learn to believe. At least, such is an understanding of this doctrine that is finding increasing favour among Catholic theologians not of the Roman school.

Rather than tying down the notion of apostolic succession to the magical-sounding and historically-dubious assertion that certain bishops have a genuine claim to be the true successors of the apostles because of a laying-on-of-hands coming down to them from the twelve through an unbroken chain of such commissionings, theologians like Hans Küng would see the Christian communities themselves as being primarily in the apostolic succession.

They would claim that the scriptural and historical evidence points to such a view. In the first place, it seems clear from the New Testament that those who were called to preside over the various churches did so as a service to their particular community, and that they were originally appointed in differing ways. In the churches founded by Peter or those under the influence of the

Jewish Christians of Palestine, groups of *bishops*, generally chosen by the community, were commissioned by means of a Jewish ceremony that denoted the handing-on of the office of rabbi – that is, by a laying-on-of-hands. But the Pauline churches at first seem to have ordered things somewhat differently and much more loosely. For them, it was sufficient that a man felt the *call* to join the group of *prophets* (not bishops) that presided over each church, and that he was *accepted* as such by his community. Indeed, this charismatic form of the ministry of Word and sacrament only fell into disuse when the danger arose of confusing the Christian prophet with his gnostic counterpart.

Under this threat, Paul's churches, too, adopted the episcopal system. We might add here, however, that the very existence of a prophetic ministry in the New Testament Church means that such a way of receiving what Roman Catholics would now call *holy orders* is just as traditional as the methods of ordination and consecration current in episcopal churches today.

Since, into the bargain, the Roman Catholic Church now officially admits that other Christian bodies are genuine churches, one might well ask whether, from Rome's viewpoint, such churches might not be recognised as having an authentic eucharistic ministry – or, indeed, whether (since the eucharist makes the Church) they could exist at all as churches without it. However much they may misunderstand its true meaning, what they basically desire is the eucharist of Christ and not another. To that end, they *accept* as ministers men who themselves feel *called* to such an office. May not these therefore be regarded as charismatic or prophetic ministers in the Pauline sense?

Even with the ending of the Pauline form of ministry in New Testament times, still the Church continued, here and there, to dispense with any laying-on-of-hands, for it seems certain that bishops and even patriarchs were sometimes appointed in the next two centuries by the choice of the people and their own acceptance of that choice. And priests were occasionally ordained by fellow-priests well into the late medieval period.

Furthermore, if we are to judge the genuineness of the eucharist by the orthodoxy of the community's or minister's eucharistic theology, then there may well be many a Catholic mass, today as well as in the past, that would have to be judged as wanting on that score. If Protestants have tended to be minimalist on questions like the eucharistic presence and sacrifice, have not Catholics equally tended to be maximalist? And which is the greater error – to believe too little or too much?

Should we not rather say that, in either case, what was primarily desired, despite any secondary misconceptions, was plainly the eucharist that Jesus wished his followers to celebrate? And that such an intention, with a minister properly designated, in either the episcopal or the prophetic form, to preside over the celebration, guarantees to any Christian gathering an authentic eucharist? It is obvious that such an opinion, if tenable, has wide ecumenical implications, with regard, for example, to the question of Anglican orders and to the even more momentous problem of intercommunion.

However, the prophets were in fact replaced by bishops even within Paul's own lifetime. And then, two further developments took place.

First, the group of bishops in each church tended to be whittled down to one. This gradual emergence of a *monarchical episcopate* may be put down partially to the paternalistic temper of the times, when a single father-figure would seem more suitable and sensible to the local community; but even more to the growing spirit of clericalisation we have already noted, and the tendency to equate the bishop with the high priest of the Old Testament.

Secondly, the claim of the Christian churches to be the successors of the apostles had to be reinforced in opposition to the gnostics' counter-claim of their having received another, secret message from John the evangelist or from some other source. It no longer seemed sufficient merely to say in reply that the faith of the individual churches was perfectly reliable because it had first been preached to them by one of the apostles. Instead, the claim came to be made, even in communities where this was not demonstrably so, that each individual bishop had received his own authority to preach the authentic Christian gospel by means of a line of consecrations that derived from an apostle.

Nor was such an over-simplification without any foundation. It expressed in a mythical way the bishop's very real claim to belong within the apostolic succession precisely because, irrespective of any break in the chain of the imposing of hands that may or may not have occurred, he presided over an apostolic church as spokesman, witness and guide to its apostolic faith in Jesus, the apostolic Word.

And this was true, too, of the Roman church. Brought into being by the preaching of Peter and Paul, it was looked upon as being, in a special way, Peter's own community. Therefore its bishop came to be seen as in some way the inheritor of Peter's position as Abraham of the new Israel and rock of the whole Church of Christ.

But what is this rock-like and apostolic function of the various churches, of their bishops and of the pope of Rome? Primarily, it is to witness to the utter reliability of the Word that the Church as a whole has received via the preaching of the apostles.

The church communities are meant to show their firm conviction that, despite any dangers and difficulties and misunderstandings that might beset them, the risen Lord is with them still and will never fail to support and uphold them throughout their trials. Indeed, the individual communities are to act as rocks in giving strength and hope not only to their own members but also to their fellow-churches. And, as the first-century *Epistle of Clement* clearly shows, in matters of doubt and confusion it was to the Christians of Rome, in whose name the deacon Clement wrote his answering letter, that the other churches, in this case even in Africa, would finally turn for help.

This witness by the Christian bodies to the truth that Christ will never fail his Church was later to be understood in the western Catholic tradition as *the infallibility of the believing Church*. Indeed, however much that doctrine may have been extended, this would seem to be its basic and most important meaning.

On top of this, the bishops are called to lead their flocks by their own apostolic witness. In other words, they are to show, particularly in their preaching and giving of guidance, that they, too, believe in the unfailing presence of Jesus the Word within the community by offering encouragement to the faithful and inspiring them with hope and joy as they struggle together to understand the meaning of the gospel in the face of circumstances that will often be difficult and trying.

Individually with regard to their own churches, and together or collegially with regard to the universal Church of Christ, the bishops are meant primarily to give this rock-like and apostolic witness to the presence of that firm and enduring rock beneath our feet that is Jesus Christ himself. But the primate, the first in the field in this service of inspiring faith, is the bishop of Peter's church, who, as well as renewing a faith like Peter's in the hearts of Christians everywhere, confirms his brother bishops when they, too, falter and become afraid.

Again, this would seem to be the most important way of understanding a doctrine that has come to be expressed, in the Roman Catholic Church, as *the infallibility of the teaching Church* – that is, of the bishops acting in communion with one another and with the bishop of Rome, and of the pope alone in his role of confirmer or strengthener of the faith of all his brethren.

Faith, in this basic sense, means a conscious adherence to Christ. It is that complete trust in the saving presence of Jesus in our world that is foundational to the Church. But faith also produces creeds.

In making the presence of Christ his Word known to the Church, God is revealing not truths but *the* truth who is Jesus. As Gabriel Moran has put it, 'though the truths men speak may be revealing of God, no *truths* have been revealed by God'. For the statements the Church goes on to formulate about this Word of truth are themselves but historical and human attempts to put its faith into intelligible propositions couched in the language and thought-forms of a particular culture and period.

In this effort at understanding, it is the task of the bishops to help the community articulate its beliefs as well as may be by guiding and expressing and making considered judgements upon the Christian inquiry. Thus the idea behind *ecumenical councils* is that the bishops of the entire Church gather together to witness to the faith of their particular churches in order that, out of this pooled evidence, a more correct and adequate way of putting the gospel teaching may be discerned for the benefit of Christians everywhere. Similarly, in *papal definitions*, the bishop of Rome, though acting individually, gives witness to the faith not just of the Roman but of the world-wide Church.

For the episcopal task in making authoritative statements about Christian belief is to encourage and give renewed hope to the faithful in their endeavours by reminding them that the Church can never lose its hold upon the truth who is Christ. This does not mean, however, that it completely understands him, but rather that he is the sure foundation that ever underpins the Christian community in its struggle to increase what little understanding it already has.

Though we may say that the doctrine of the infallibility of the Church, an infallibility that is shared, too, by the college of bishops and by the pope, expresses in legalistic and jurisdictional terms the basic fact that Jesus is the rock upon whom all Christians should rely, yet infallibility is also understood among Roman Catholics as applying especially to verbal formulae, to those statements of doctrine that have been put forward with the gravest solemnity by the highest teaching authority of the Church. But how is the assertion that certain sets of words are guaranteed by God as completely free from doctrinal error to be saved from the accusation of being magical and preposterous?

Hans Küng would say that it cannot. For him, infallibility simply means that the whole Christian Church is indefectible in truth despite all its errors and mistakes. In witnessing to the un-failing presence of Christ, in his Holy Spirit, in the Church, the teaching authority vested in the bishops and above all in the pope will make statements for the guidance of the community that, however authoritative their presentation, may in fact be wrong.

To Küng, infallibility is not a quality to be attached to certain kinds of proposition, whether these are the ancient creeds, the solemn teaching of councils or the dogmatic proclamations of individual popes. While these may well be true explicitations of the gospel, they should not, in his view, be spoken of as infallible, as though declarations of this kind could never be incorrect.

This is not to say that such statements should not be treated with great respect. As attempts to articulate the beliefs of the Christian Church and in order to reassure it that Christ is the ultimate and enduring security underlying it throughout all its mistakes and despite all its errors, the teachings of the early councils, for instance, before the great schism between east and west, are particularly valuable, since truly representative of the whole Church of their day. After the schism, the councils of western Christendom are still of immense value but have less weight in that they represent a more one-sided view, while the conciliar and papal teachings of the post-reformation period will be inclined to be even more partial since representing largely a mediterranean understanding of the gospel which failed to take into account that of the whole Church of Christ.

Without discarding the traditional Christian teachings that represent our forefathers' struggles to grasp the meaning of the Word of God, Küng feels that it is unnecessary to treat such formulations as infallible and irreformable. Much better, he declares, to admit that statements of popes and councils, bishops and theologians have sometimes been wrong in the past and will sometimes be wrong in the future, and to relocate infallibility in Christ the rock of the Church and in the task of the apostolic ministry (and above all the Petrine ministry) within the Church to help us place all our trust more firmly upon our Lord despite the confusion, the mistakes and the uncertainties that our continuing effort at understanding Christianity better is bound to engender.

Such a view, though liberating to some Roman Catholics, is distressing to others and certainly cannot be squared with the attitude of the Roman authorities or of the school of theology this attitude reflects, which fixes infallibility very firmly upon certain types of doctrinal proposition. Nevertheless, there are other theologians who, though uncomfortable with the more rigid explanation, find Küng's solution altogether too extreme.

While agreeing that infallibility could be the better translated as 'indefectibility in truth', and seeing the apostolic ministry vested in pope and bishops as primarily concerned with showing Christians how to renew their trust in Jesus as their corner-stone, yet they would go on to assert that, in the last resort and in matters of great moment, this teaching authority cannot lead the Church irrevocably astray or commit it fundamentally to error. For, in such a case, the Christ who is always present through his Spirit in the Christian community would have failed as a rock of reliance and would, in fact, have let the Church down drastically.

Nevertheless, this is far from saying that the Church's infallible teachings are always perfectly phrased and incapable of being improved upon. Since no definition can grasp and pin down in words the whole truth that is Christ, then every statement, be it never so inerrant, will be inadequate and partial as an expression of Christian belief, and to that extent will be unbalanced and misleading. In other words, conciliar and papal teachings demand exegesis. One must go into their provenance, into the circumstances, the ways of thinking, the presuppositions and the culture out of which they grew if one would discover what they are really saying, and not merely what they seem to say when taken in twentieth-century terms and divorced from their historical background.

Even then, however, questions keep cropping up which make the recognition of what are infallible statements a less easy task than the hard-liners of the Roman school would imply. For instance, the question of the value of ecumenical councils after the schism still remains. Since these failed to give full representation to the eastern churches, whose orders and ecclesial status have never been seriously denied by Rome, in what sense can they be held to be representative of the whole Church and their decrees as weighty and as binding as, say, the councils of Ephesus, Chalcedon or Nicaea? Certainly, the recognition by Vatican II of a hierarchy of truths would justify one in seeing these early councils as of more fundamental importance than the later assemblies, without necessarily denying that the definitions of the latter, however poorly phrased, were nevertheless free from doctrinal error.

Again, the 1870 definition of papal infallibility stresses that the pope is endowed with the same infallibility bequeathed by Christ to his Church, but only when, as shepherd and teacher of all Christians, he proposes for their belief an article of faith or morals as part of the gospel of the Lord. But Roman Catholicism has a wider view today of the Church than it had at Vatican I, and sees it as subsisting not merely within the Roman communion but also in the other Christian churches. This brings up the question as to how the whole Church can be thus infallible, despite the differences of opinion displayed by the various churches in their statements of faith, and even more how the bishop of Rome may be said to act as that wider Church's shepherd and guide. May not both assertions of infallibility be taken to mean simply that Christ is the ever-present rock of the whole divided and apparently crumbling Christian community, and that the ministry of Peter is meant to speak *for* that whole Church and *to* it in order to restore to it, in the face of its divisions, confidence and hope in the Lord?

If we take Hans Küng's propositions seriously, a further question, and one that he himself only hints at, inevitably poses itself. It is this. Let us assume we accept the contention that the infallibility of the teaching ministry in the Church, and of the Petrine ministry in particular, is but a halting, outmoded way of saying that the true role of the whole teaching ministry is to confirm the rest of the Church by reminding it that, despite all its errors and failings, the Word of God is in its midst. Do we therefore need to go on from there to claim that this ministry is necessarily and exclusively linked to particular institutions? In other words, is it a ministry that is to be found only among the bishops, and above all with the incumbent of the Roman see? While all would admit that the bishops can indeed fail in their ministry, could we not also admit that the same ministry may also be found at work among other Christians in a charismatic, prophetical way? Perhaps Francis of Assisi or Martin Luther King were exercising the ministry of Peter in the Church of God more authentically than, say, Pope Alexander VI?

Even theologians who cannot accept Hans Küng's extreme position, much less its further implications, are nevertheless themselves reassessing the doctrine of infallibility in their own terms. Where their enquiries will lead, or how far the results will be in line with the gospel and acceptable both to the authorities and faithful of their own church and to their fellow-Christians in the other churches remains to be seen. But one thing is certain – we have no need to fear such an enquiry. For the Spirit of Christ is with the Church. It can never fail.

Indeed, this points, it would seem to me, to the particular vocation of the Roman Catholic Church in the ecumenical endeavour of the present time. As the Petrine community in a special way, it should surely be the first to give an example of the faith of Peter in the Christ as Son of the living God and corner-stone of the Church. It should be the first to inspire all Christians with hope and encourage them to trust in the Lord in the face of the disappointments and apparently insuperable difficulties that they face today. It should, at the same time, and by reason of its own long history summed up in its ancient institution of the papacy, invite other Christians to take a deeper look at their common heritage and at the traditional ways of understanding the gospel that were arrived at by their forefathers in the faith.

Thus the role of the Roman Catholic Church, and of the Catholic communities, their bishops and the Roman pope is basically to present Jesus Christ to the world as the one rock of security for all mankind and for every Christian, and the man upon whom the future of the whole human race is firmly grounded and fixed. If, in doing so, the Church seeks to express certain truths about this fundamental faith in the Word of God, it is not claiming thereby that its bishops, in Rome or elsewhere, are oracles whose utterances are directly inspired from on high, but that its spokesmen are finally to be trusted precisely and only because Christ himself is to be trusted.

6

THE MEANING OF MEDITATION

THE WHOLE Church is at present very much divided over the question of prayer. On the one hand, there are those who would put down every trouble besetting our Christian communities today – in particular such facts as decreasing congregations, the continuing decline in vocations to the ministry or the growing number of clergy and religious who are leaving their professions – to a loss of the sense of prayer. On the other hand, many Christians are genuinely anxious to discover what prayer can really mean in the modern world. They fear that, when they pray, they may simply be talking to themselves or toying with day-dreams while children meanwhile starve and nations are oppressed and human beings exploit and kill each other.

Certainly, the habit of pray*ing* is going steadily to disappear from the lives of those who doubt the value and meaning of pray*er*. And yet, I would suggest, their questioning attitude is far more healthy than that of the Christian who sees no problem in pray*er* as such, however difficult he may admit the actual practice of pray*ing* to be.

It is in order to help the former, therefore, and to disturb the latter that I should like to set down some ways of understanding prayer that are current in the churches today.

But first, it would be useful if we were to group all the elements that make up Christian prayer under the two headings of *meditation* and *petition*. By meditation I would mean in general those ways in which we prepare ourselves mentally and emotionally for what are traditionally classified as acts of adoration, thanksgiving, contrition, intercession and petition, but which can all in fact be seen as petitionary in the sense in which many Christians are coming now to understand that term. This is not to say, however, that the meditative and the petitionary aspects of prayer can really be separated one from the other. On the contrary, prayer as meditation always finally includes some kind of petitioning, and prayer as petition always begins by being meditative in some way.

Indeed, meditation would fail to be prayer without this vital element of petition. It follows therefore that the whole enterprise of praying would be judged a waste of time if one were to doubt, as many do today, the worth of petitioning as such. Thus it is with the problem of prayer as petition that this survey will begin.

1. Prayer as Petition

We are taught by the gospels to speak familiarly with our God. We are told to thank him for past benefits, to love him for his goodness, to seek his forgiveness and to ask for his favours. And yet we are often hesitant to do so. We find it rather pointless to tell him things he already knows, whether about himself, about our own attitudes, or about the things we need.

Yet Jesus tells us that whatever we ask for we shall receive. And, if at first we don't succeed, that we must keep on trying.

But it doesn't always work out that way. Ask as often as we will, we may still not get what we want. In any case, we rightly feel reticent about repeatedly petitioning the Almighty, for we know that we cannot really expect, when we pray for such things as sunshine or success in exams, that God is going to alter the weather pattern of the whole earth in our favour (and despite the requests to the contrary he has also without doubt received), or to give us an unfair advantage over our competitors in the examination room. And we feel that it smacks of the magical to imagine that, if we keep on asking, God is bound to grant us our wish in the end. Yet the parable of the man who, at midnight, keeps on knocking at his friend's door until the latter eventually gets up out of bed to answer him seems to be saying just that.

However, such an understanding over-simplifies the whole New Testament teaching on prayer. True, the words of Jesus in the gospels, as they sound out an encouragement to pray, will inevitably do so in the only terms their hearers will be able, with their background, to accept and grasp—that is, by using the language of human requesting or by means of the picture of a God who listens like a human monarch to what we have to say and gives in if we go on at him for long enough.

But we should always hear in the background and behind such ways of speaking about prayer the more important words, 'Thy will be done.' For it is this truth that makes all the difference between prayer of the Christian and of the magical variety. As Jan Peters puts it:

'Christian prayer in the New Testament is pre-eminently altruistic and concentrates on God's will as effectively tending towards the salvation of his people, at every level. It sharply rejects the pagan prayer which tries to make the gods come round to one's own views (*fatigare deos*). In contrast, Christian prayer makes clear that prayer is not the same as exorcising the power of the divinity but rather the expression in faith of that real impotence which besets man when he listens to the sermon on the mount and when he realises that the kingdom of God will come as salvation and not as a matter of force and fate' (*Concilium*, February, 1970).

Prayer as petition does not therefore ask for miracles or expect God to act as the great problem-solver. It cannot, in other words, excuse man from trying to discover how to solve his own problems in this world. What it does do, however, is to help him to see them in the light of the gospel, and indeed to become more fully aware of his position in relation to God and his kingdom. And it does so because it introduces him more fully into the consciousness of Christ.

It was by the Word that was once preached to us, the good news we have received in faith, that we first came to know that our love of other people is in fact the love of God, for it puts us into relationship with him as children with a Father since it is the love, or Holy Spirit, of his Son. And it is precisely this Spirit of love that is the reign of God, by means of which he wills to establish his kingdom in the hearts of human beings.

In the prayer of faith, we become more conscious of the Word we have received. We recognise Christ's presence with us when we gather ourselves together in his name, and we acknowledge afresh and with greater intensity the message of salvation in his Spirit that he came to bring. Thus, in prayer, we participate in Christ's own loving *awareness* of God as his Father and of all human beings as his brothers and sisters.

Conscious, then, of our relationship with God and men, we become conscious, too, of its weakness and inadequacy. We come to realise, in comparison with the example Jesus gave us, how ineffective and frail is our loving and that, of ourselves, we can do nothing.

Thus we are led on to make the fundamental petition, 'Thy kingdom come, They will be done.' Whether by recognising with gratitude and wonder the love God has revealed to us in Christ, by coming with regret to see how far we have failed its demands, by resolving to face up more courageously to the difficulties that hamper our efforts at fellowship or by renewing our trust that the reign of brotherhood and peace will come about in the end, even though the problems that beset it are at present beyond our powers of coping – in all these ways we shall be helping to bring about the kingdom by changing, not the mind of God, but our own attitude in its favour.

Thus genuine prayer is always answered. Not only is it expressive, that is to say, of a real desire that God's kingdom should come in our own lives and our own world, but it also helps bring about what it desires. For it puts into words our increased purpose of strengthening our relationships with the human community and with the God upon whose Spirit, freely given in Christ our Lord, we so utterly rely. But thus to help on the movement towards fellowship among men by opening up our hearts a little more to this Spirit of love is to help on the coming of the kingdom, the communion of saints. By drawing us more into line

D

with God's changeless purpose that the future he has revealed in Christ should be established through our co-operation, prayer turns us into more effective agents of the kingdom and, through us, brings the full realisation of what we pray for that much nearer.

Faced with insights of this kind, however, many Christians are becoming steadily more dissatisfied with some of the traditional formulations of prayer. When they pray, they do not want in any way to sound as though they were pagans expecting their gods to intervene on their behalf so that their own will might be done, nor as though they thought the kingdom would come about by a series of stupendous wonders. Rather, they seek to stand before God with a heightened awareness of the needs he expects them to meet in this world if his kingdom is ever to come, of their own inadequacies and their failure to respond to such needs in the past, and with a deepening desire to remedy that lack in the future while remaining utterly reliant upon God as giver of the kingdom-that-is-coming in the resurrection of Jesus his Son.

One example of an attempt at restating in non-magical and in up-to-date terms this Christian reality of prayer as petition is to be found in the seven theses used as guidelines by an ecumenical group in Cologne in arranging the special services it has named *Political Vespers*. These vespers begin with information that outlines some theme of special relevance to the setting up of God's kingdom today. It may explore the question of aid to the Third World, the war in Vietnam or the situation in Greece, but whatever topic it takes is examined thoroughly and pondered upon in the light of the Christian message with the aid of Bible readings, prayers, meditation and singing. But the outcome of the service is meant always to be a decision for action, with the group trying to discover ways in which it can help to uproot this particular injustice or help this particular cause, and so promote the kingdom in this particular way.

The theses of the *Political Vespers* group are as follows:

1. Christian prayer renounces miracles.
2. Prayer prepares man to accept responsibility for his world.

The actions of men will not be replaced by the action of God.

3. In prayer man accepts responsibility for the condition of his world. He is only able to accept responsibility for what he knows and perceives. Therefore *information is the first stage of prayer*.

4. In a non-authoritarian community, it will not be a case of some giving information and others receiving it. Exact knowledge of the situation will be searched for by people together weighing the arguments. Therefore *the second stage of prayer is exposition, discussion*.

5. Prayer makes us conscious of what is not yet, but will be brought on by us. Therefore *discussion of the possibilities of action belongs to it as a third stage*.

6. In verbalising prayer, man formulates himself in the sight of God, in his pain about the kingdom still absent, in his hope of this kingdom, in his responsibility for bringing it on. In prayer, man takes charge of God's business as his own.

7. Even where man cannot be helped any more by men, and where he cannot act any more, there prayer keeps alive in him hunger for the kingdom of God, makes him more human in his *not-being-satisfied*, and prevents him from giving up hope of making sense of the world.

It is significant that this particular move towards making prayer more acceptable to modern, western man should take the form of group intercession, and that the rejection of less adequate ways of understanding intercessory prayer has not, in fact, meant the rejection of the old idea of prayer as a community endeavour. Indeed, it seeks very much to restore this communal perspective and to assert that we may well pray best when gathered together with our fellow-Christians.

All too often, the common prayer of Christians has meant little more than that of a conglomeration of strangers gathered under one roof to recite in unison prayer formulae already long composed and perhaps with little relevance to their own individual experiences, or else to say their amens to someone giving voice to concerns and preoccupations that are his rather than theirs.

Prayer that springs from the heart of a real community, however, and that expresses, in an informal and spontaneous way, the desire for the kingdom of a more or less closely knit group of friends or acquaintances will tend to gain in quality. Since prayer explains to us how we stand before God by letting us see more clearly how we stand within the human community, then communal prayer ought to do so more effectively as the activity of a group to which we are bound in relationships of which we are at that moment very conscious. The group is thus the microcosm of the human race for us, and our attitude towards it a faithful reflection of our attitude towards mankind as a whole. Since this attitude of ours towards the human community and the degree to which we are contributing to its growth in fellowship in turn defines our real attitude towards God, then the experience of praying with this particular group should be of great benefit in helping us strengthen our loving union with the Father by encouraging us to renew our efforts at loving other people.

Mark Gibbard has summarised this advantage of group prayer in an article that appeared with that of Jan Peters in the issue of *Concilium* already quoted.

'Nowadays, in many places the small informal group is very effective in helping people discover what prayer really is. This is not the traditional prayer-circle long familiar in many churches. It is a mixed group consisting partly of those with some experience of prayer and partly of inquirers and seekers. They need to come to know one another sufficiently well to share their convictions and experiences freely and humbly. . . . These groups promote openness and mutual trust. One of the common hindrances to growth in prayer is lack of good interpersonal relationships. St Thomas Aquinas has a perceptive sentence in *Contra Gentiles*: "For a man to be open to divine things he needs tranquillity and peace; now mutual love, more than anything else, removes the obstacles to peace." '

Thus the inner harmony of the group, the pooling of insights with regard to present obstacles to the setting-up of the kingdom and the common endeavour to do something about overcoming them, all these make of modern moves towards a renewed form of community prayer an exciting and helpful development.

From all that has been said, it should be clear that, to escape the danger of becoming magical, the element of petition in Christian prayer must be seen as helping to change, not God's will, but our own lives, in teaching us to accept the responsibility for changing our world in accord with that will as revealed to us in Jesus. At the same time, it will remind us that, without God, we are powerless to bring about this kingdom which, after all, has only been promised to us by the free gift of God when, in raising his Son from the dead, he showed us what our own future could be like.

Perhaps Peters could best bring this examination of the petitionary aspect of prayer to a close in a further passage from his article on prayer.

'The Church prays truly wherever the people of God pray as suggested above, where the Christian community is aware of its impotence to achieve the kingdom of God in our present culture, where Christians see themselves as "only apprentices of the gospel". Whether this takes place in a particular framework, in a "sacred" building, according to an official formula or in the family, in groups, or through the spontaneous creativity of the faithful is secondary in so far as prayer is concerned. . . . All these forms are but variations on the basic theme of man, conscious of his inadequacy in the context of his faith. That this experience of his limitations now differs from that of the Middle Ages and lies now in the direction of a Church of the poor or in the obvious need for political commitment is of secondary importance. What counts is that the Christian today sees these new limitations also in the light of the gospel.'

2. Prayer as Meditation

Christian meditation is the enterprise of paying greater attention to God and coming to recognise more forcibly that, though ultimately quite beyond our understanding, he has revealed him-

self, in the resurrection of Christ, as a God who is ever present
with us and leading us on, in the love of the Spirit, to our full
participation in the glory, the freedom and the fellowship of Jesus.

Meditation encourages *experience*. That is to say, it is a practical
exercise that is meant to help us become more fully aware of our
relationships with God, what they are and what they could become. It endeavours to let us taste and savour something of the
love of God and the bond that links us with the Absolute. In order
to do so, it employs techniques of various kinds, mystical ways or
spiritual exercises that are aimed at helping us psychologically and
emotionally to become more attentive to ourselves, our neighbours and our Father in heaven.

Experience is meant to lead into an *examination* of these relationships of ours with God and men so that we might improve
upon them and make them more useful for the service of the
kingdom. In other words, meditative prayer has as its object the
fuller development within us of true petitionary prayer. For it
prepares the ground so that we might more convincingly pray
that God's will may be done and his kingdom come in our own
lives and through our own attitudes.

Christian meditation does not, therefore, seek experience for
experience's sake. It is not meant simply to provide us with a
pleasing religious sensation. Neither does it give us any guarantee
that the psychological states we undergo necessarily reflect our
real situation before God. For the true assessment of the depth of
our union with him is to be found precisely in assessing the way
we fit into the community and to what extent we really do try to
love our neighbour. Meditation merely provides us with some
evidence of what our tentative and inadequate union with God
really means, and of what it could and should become.

Explanations of meditative ways or techniques that see sensation, however, as an end in itself are strictly non-Christian.
Though the methods they propose and the psychological effects
these produce will be largely identical with those known to the
Christian tradition, yet the purpose for which they are sought
really vitiates them. Meditation becomes then a way of escape

from the everyday world rather than a means for transforming it, and mysticism is consequently turned into a bromide, a drug.

Indeed, such a pursuit is typical of occult meditation. As Duncan observes in *The Christ, Psychotherapy and Magic*, 'Above all else, occultism stands or falls by the *experience* it provides. In everything experience is the criterion; in ceremonial magic, in solitary meditation, it is always experience that is sought. The occultist is one who, deliberately and seriously, "lives for kicks" because the "kicks" are, to him, all part and parcel of the Great Work of enlarging his consciousness to the power of infinity.'

But the occultist is not the only species of mystic to believe that the experience of increased awareness, of the expanding of consciousness or the blowing of one's mind is in fact the goal of human living and the fullest and most real encounter with the Absolute that is possible to any creature on this earth. Such an idea is common to much eastern spirituality and to the hippy mystics of our modern drug sub-culture. And it is also to be found, as we have seen in an earlier chapter, cropping up again and again in the Christian mystical tradition.

And it threatens the Church today. On the one hand, there are those Christians who would claim that the means they employ, whether taken up from Walter Hilton, John of the Cross or Zen Buddhism, lead them to a kind of union with God that they cannot achieve in their ordinary daily living. On the other, there are those who, in Christian adaptations of the methods of the T-groups or the Esalen Institute, seek experience in sensitivity and self-awareness within their group encounters that they would hold to be a far more real meeting with God than is to be found in less intimate and more humdrum ways of serving other people. Thus they turn what is often a very helpful process in the discovery of self and of God into a self-centred addiction to the experience of free expression for its own sake.

While reminding ourselves that the pursuit of this heightened awareness of self and God as an end in itself is strictly an anti-Christian occupation and a magical flight from the real world that Jesus would never have commended, nevertheless we need to reassert today that meditation still has value for the Christian. Indeed, today's young are actually helping towards a revival of meditation in the churches.

For, in fact, meditative prayer has always held an honoured place in Christianity – though often honoured more in the breach than in the observance. Indeed, the strain is particularly strong in eastern Orthodoxy and western Catholicism. But, whereas Roman Catholic mystical theology has managed in this century finally to escape from its infatuation with the élitist idea that meditation produces a depth of union with God impossible outside of prayer, its practices are still often so embedded in past forms and outworn patterns as to have lost much of their spark and spontaneity.

Today, however, young people are finding more helpful ways of becoming aware, ways that we should not reject as untraditional but rather, where they fulfil their purpose in a wholesome manner, welcome as ways of reviving meditative prayer. Gerard Broccolo reminded us of this in a recent article on *The Priest Praying in the Midst of the Family of Man.*

'In the McLuhan era of non-verbal, mass media communications, mechanically produced sights and sounds are being introduced, and rightly so, into the devotional life of (especially) our younger Christians. Consequently, we occasionally notice paraliturgical services which are almost psychedelic in form and most timely in content, e.g. themes of loneliness, estrangement, the need for fraternal reconciliation, etc. But so long as a truly Christian vision or orientation is present, these new forms of prayer can have the same spiritual value for today's Christian as the older devotions had for his counterpart in the past' (*Concilium*, February 1970).

While older meditative techniques are too much wedded to the printed page and the spoken word to suit an electronic and less letter-bound age, the spoken word can nevertheless still prove of great help in group meditation, and I should like now to describe one such attempt at evolving a modern and appealing form of meditation that nevertheless relies very heavily upon the words of the group leader. Indeed, I would add by way of commendation that I have used this method with groups of all ages, from students to elderly nuns, and that the majority of the participants have found the experience most impressive – as I have myself. It is a method that is solidly based on old Christian practices, and yet has strong affinities with some of the basic techniques of yoga and of Zen, and is one to which, in the form I now present it, I was myself first introduced by Kathleen Gabb, a Christian catechist working largely among teenagers.

The meditation begins with an exercise in self-composure that is meant to induce calm and peace of mind before going on to stimulate a greater awareness of oneself in relation to humanity, the universe and God: and it ends by leading into the prayer of petition as we have already defined it. In other words, and to use the coinage of Catholic meditational practice, it begins with *composition of place and time* and ends with *affections and resolutions*!

(a) Attention

The group should be sitting comfortably and preferably in a darkened, quiet and airy room. As a prelude to the exercise, soft music could well be played to help induce a feeling of peace and a freedom from tension.

Then the leader may begin, speaking slowly, softly and calmly, and pausing for anything up to a minute after making his requests.

'Sit comfortably. Place your feet firmly upon the floor. Place the palms of your hands downwards upon your knees and let them rest there gently. Let your eyes rest upon a spot on the floor just in front of your own feet. Forget your worries and anxieties and just relax.

'Feel the floor on the soles of your feet.

'Feel your hands resting upon your knees.

'Feel the pressure of the seat and the back of the chair upon your body.

'Feel the weight of the clothes on your body.

'Feel the air brushing against your face and hands.

'Without looking up, become aware of every single person and of all the objects present in this room.

'Listen to the sounds that are farthest away from you.

'Listen to the sounds that are nearest.

'Listen to your own breathing. Become conscious of its rhythm as the breath is drawn into your lungs and expelled again.

'Listen to the beating of your own heart. Become aware of its regularity as it pumps the blood round your body.'

(b) Composure

This time, the silence after each invitation should last longer, for about three minutes. The leader begins:

'Breath regularly, in and out, in and out.

'As you breath in, draw in "peace" (or "good" or "love" or simply "Jesus").

'As you breath out, breath out "worry" (or "guilt" or "hate" or "self").

'Now, as you breath in, continue to breath in peace, etc., and as you breath out imagine that this peace is going right down into the depths of your heart. Breath in peace, let it sink into your heart. Breath in peace, let it sink into your heart.'

(c) Expansion of Consciousness

This is the psychedelic or mind-enlarging part of the procedure. Again, the leader should pause for about a minute after each suggestion, and for ten seconds or so at the spaces indicated by dots.

'You are sitting in a room in a house in (name the road or locality).

'Picture to yourself not only this room but all the other rooms in the house, upstairs and downstairs. Go through them all in your imagination.

'Picture the outside of the house . . . what it looks like from the front . . . from the back . . . from the air.

'This house is one of many houses and buildings that make up (name the town or district).

'The town to which you belong is built upon (a little geographical or geological information here, e.g. "the clay banks of the Thames estuary", "the immemorial limestone rocks of the Yorkshire dales").

'It is set upon a small island, surrounded by the sea. Picture to yourself an overall view of the British Isles to which you belong.

'This island of yours is fixed, with many other continents and islands, upon the planet Earth. Imagine how your planet looks from outer space. Remember how it looked to the astronauts on the moon – like a blue and glittering globe hanging in the blackness of infinity.

'This earth of ours is spinning through space as it circles round the sun.

'This sun is one of the many millions of burning stars that go to make up our galaxy. This galaxy of ours is ever turning as it moves through boundless space.

'Our galaxy is one of countless millions of galaxies, all of them wheeling perpetually on and on through limitless space.'

(d) Practical Outcome

One can now reintroduce the theme that originally concerned the prayer-group. This may have to be spelled out again in some detail, or may be left for the group to remember in relation to what they have just experienced and to apply to their own lives and attitudes.

For example, the leader could simply say, 'Who *am* I?', leaving a pause of anything up to five minutes before going on to ask, '*Whose* am I?' However, he may, after a further pause of similar length, go on to mention more specifically our relationship with God and with each other, and the demands made upon us by God and the community with regard to the particular problem the group is praying about.

After a much longer period of silence, lasting for perhaps twenty minutes or more, the leader could then suggest some kind of short formula that would sum up the group's attitude – perhaps a scripture sentence like 'Whatsoever you do to the least of my brothers, that you do unto me', to be repeated slowly by the group, either silently and for a number of times, or aloud and perhaps even sung or chanted. Or he and others in the group might instead compose longer prayers expressive of the concern of the members.

Although this is simply a suggestion of one way in which meditation can come alive for ordinary Christians in the latter half of the twentieth century, it is one that manages, I think fairly successfully, to take up and reinterpret traditional techniques of prayer while at the same time showing quite clearly that prayer as meditation has for its very purpose prayer as petition. Instead of gratifying, soothing and lulling the one who prays into the kind of security afforded to men by magic and mystery, Christian prayer in all its aspects is thus meant to send its practitioners back into the world with a greater awareness that Christ waits for them there and relies on their help in establishing the kingdom of his Father in the community of men.

7

ALTERNATIVE SOCIETIES

ONE OF the more striking features of present-day life in the west is the growth of what might be called the *community movement*, from the hippy colonies of southern California to the socialist communes of Scandinavia, and the demands of peoples like the Basques or Welsh or Scots to be treated as national groups with an identity of their own.

There is a parallel movement going on, too, in the western churches, from the endeavour to create a worshipping community out of the medieval institution of the parish to experiments in team ministry and corporate living for the clergy; from family groups to ecumenical fellowships like Shalom in Holland or Political Vespers in Germany; from the impetus in the Roman Catholic communion towards a renewal of the way of life of its religious orders and congregations to the experiments in adapting this traditional form of Christian witness to the needs of the present that we see, for example, among the Anglican Societies of the Sacred Mission and of St Francis, at Taizé and Iona or with the Simon and St Mungo communities in their work among the dispossessed.

In every case, the community movement represents an act of *protest* – against western society in general, family life in the west, or western-style Christianity.

Western society seems to many to be so dominated by commercial concerns that the individual has no longer any real power to challenge or to change governmental policies formulated primarily for upholding and promoting this system. The demands of the consumer society, carefully cultivated by the great financial interests whose profits are dependent upon ever-increasing production, weigh heavily upon the family unit, which is becoming steadily more isolated and self-concerned.

The typical *western family* of mother, father and two to three children, enclosed in its own tiny home, is being perpetually bombarded and pressurised into consuming more by appeals to its greed and selfishness, so that inevitably it turns in upon itself and tends to forget about the needs of those outside its own small circle.

And the *western churches* seem so often to be tied down to their past and to be organised according to the outmoded patterns of a feudal and authoritarian society when they should instead be presenting a challenge, by their witness to the value of genuine community living, to the ills that are doing such damage to the family and to the community at the present time. On the contrary, however, they seem frequently to support the social set-up when they should be criticising it, and to be as dedicated to material interests and the pursuit of wealth as any big-business corporation.

The evils of our times against which the community movement in the west is protesting can be organised under three main headings – enforced chastity, enforced poverty and enforced obedience.

By *enforced chastity* I mean those unjust restrictions of the basic human need to love and be loved that so often go hand in hand with materialism.

The family itself is the first to suffer under the pressures of enforced chastity, since it is compelled to remain small and self-enclosed by the very size of the housing with which it is provided and of the wages it is paid, especially when these are viewed in relation to the list of goods it has been persuaded by skillful advertising that it ought to possess if it is to achieve respectability and to the consequent high cost of living in our industrialised western world. Thus the so-called nuclear family finds it increasingly difficult to care for a wider range of kin or to look with anything but suspicion upon the outsider who comes from beyond family or racial boundaries to compete for jobs and for possessions.

The tightening family circle is less able, therefore, to take in elderly or unmarried relatives, who are relegated to the apparent rejection of the old peoples' home or to a life of acute loneliness as odd and unwanted maiden aunts or bachelor uncles. The children, too, may well feel themselves somewhat neglected as the mother goes out to work to supplement the family income, while husband and wife, under constant appeals to their acquisitiveness, will find it difficult to decide objectively the number of children they ought to rear and may well find themselves involved in the tensions that can arise over the physical and psychological dangers and the moral problems created by such questions as the pill, abortion and divorce. Again, the demands of industry may separate the father from the rest of the family for periods of intolerable length. He may have to migrate to districts or countries where his dependents cannot follow in order to find suitable work. Or he may find himself on shift work or in some other occupation that requires him to be away from home for long stretches of time.

Enforced poverty, and that on ever-increasing levels, seems to be an inescapable side-effect of the running of an advanced consumer society. The pockets of real poverty in the United States and Great Britain, for example, and the alienation people feel from work that is often mere repetitive drudgery point to a certain callousness attendant upon a rich country's efforts at remaining productive and profitable, come what may. And this priority of profit is even more noticeable when we look at the Third World. It is by now a truism (though not one that the nuclear family is encouraged to recognise or that governments dare in consequence try to tackle whole-heartedly) that the rich, white nations of the world, whether capitalist or communist, are getting steadily richer largely at the expense of the non-white peoples of the earth who provide, at disastrously low and unfair prices, substantial parts of the raw material to keep the white man's factories going and his supermarkets stocked with goods. As our standard of living rises, so the Third World grows steadily and inescapably poorer. And any way it may seek to get out of its impasse will generally be threatened with forcible suppression by the white interests who stand to lose, in the short term, by the development of the peoples they exploit.

And this leads on to the evil of *enforced obedience*. Many would see commercial interests as the main factor today behind the wars the white nations wage or support in the territories of their poor neighbours, whether in Vietnam, Cambodia, the Congo, Nigeria or the Near East. Such wars of liberation seem rather to impose by force a system and an ideology that will support the financial prosperity of the western powers than to seek genuine self-determination for the 'liberated', who must pretend to become completely communist or capitalist or democratic or whatever, depending upon which army succeeds in doing the liberating first. At the same time, back in the white world, criticism of the domestic power structure will often meet with suppression under the cloak of 'law and order', while the educational system and the mass media will be geared, as far as possible, into supporting the system and disarming dissent.

The community movement makes its protest against these evils by seeking to create an alternative to society and family life in the west. And it does so in two distinct and opposing ways.

There is the way of the *drop-out*. This is the solution that was first proposed by Alan Ginsberg and taken up by the original flower-children of San Francisco, and has since produced the hippy communes. And it is the solution that has also been proposed at times by Christians, is repeated today by groups like the Children of God, and is still occasionally claimed as the motive for a person's becoming, for instance, a monk or a nun.

The hippy protest against the evils that threaten communal life in the western world does not take the form of trying to change that world or to overthrow its power-structures but simply of opting out and ignoring it.

As his own answer to enforced chastity and the way it is twisting family life, the hippy simply rejects the institution of the family as far as he possibly can. Sex, freely indulged in, is taken merely as a mutual pleasure and a mark of tenderness rather than an expression of a deeper kind of love and the desire for some kind of stable relationship between the participants. Instead, therefore, of challenging society's assumptions about the nuclear family as the natural unit out of which the national community is built, the hippy simply turns away from dialogue in order to use sexuality as a plaything, a toy, a game.

Against enforced poverty and the drudgery of meaningless work, the hippy will often simply refuse to work at all and will learn, instead, how to sponge off or steal from the system. Rather than trying to improve upon the commercial set-up that so dehumanises working people and exploits the masses of the non-white world, the drop-out tries to live by outwitting, not challenging, it.

As his reply to enforced obedience and the abuse of power by the strong, the hippy disowns all authority as far as he can. Recognising no law save the basic imperative of 'doing one's thing' and living in love and peace within the commune, and seeking experiences that will allow him to forget the harsh realities of the outside, 'straight' world, he shrinks from taking on the forces of oppression but generally prefers to flee from them and hide out in an ivory tower of his own devising, where drugs and dreams replace the light of day.

This is not to say that hippies never fall really in love or grow their own food or show concern for the ills of society or play a constructive role in protesting against injustice. It is not to say that they do not proselytise and preach the message of love and peace or seek to lead like-minded folk to adopt their way of living. But it is to affirm that, on the whole, they are marked with a negative and escapist attitude that not only shirks adult responsibility for making this world a better place to live in but also irks older generations by setting out to shock and disgust rather than to convert them.

Not that one can blame them for dropping out. The task of improving our world seems impossibly daunting, and the middle-aged immovable in their prejudices, even to the most ardent activist or left-wing revolutionary.

There can be drop-outs in convents and monasteries too. Indeed, certain kinds of spirituality have at times encouraged such an attitude, so that it often seemed as if to 'enter religion' or 'the church', to 'take the veil' or to 'make one's vows' was to 'leave the world' in the sense of rejecting it and spurning it as a place too dangerous and unworthy to be bothered about.

This attitude is in fact fairly common today – not so much among religious themselves as among the ordinary people. For it is what the religious life so often looks like in the witness of its secluded buildings, its strange dress and its odd life-style. And it is how many Christians would wish to retain it, since to imagine that there is a whole class of people especially dedicated to holiness and an other-worldly life on their behalf relieves them of their own responsibility for witnessing to Christian values in the everyday world.

Indeed, one still does come across the man or woman who treats his or her vows of chastity, poverty and obedience as ways of dropping out that are as irresponsible as those of the wildest hippy.

The vow of chastity can be taken to mean a rejection of the married state as somehow distasteful and tainted with impurity, or to embody a refusal to come to terms with and rejoice over one's own sexuality or to enter upon the risk and responsibility of truly loving other people. The life of a person who is afraid not only of the fact of human sexuality but also of all human affection and comradeship, has itself become less than human in its icy aloofness. Furthermore, a life free from the demands of spouse or children will readily, unless balanced by a greater openness to the demands of others, turn selfish and sour.

The vow of poverty can also be made use of as a way of escape. To enter a religious order can become the means for avoiding the daily drudgery of a full day's work and evading the normal necessity of providing for oneself and one's dependents. It can, in fact, mean the adoption of the leisured life-style of Victorian gentlefolk rather than an identification with the twentieth-century poor.

The vow of obedience can come as a welcome relief to the inadequate person who shuns the responsibility of being fully human and adult as a contributing member of society. To hand over the direction of one's life completely to another, and wait to be told what to do all the time is to revert to one's childhood and to deprive the community of the fruits of one's own creativity and initiative and talents.

However, there are other, more positive ways of protesting against the sicknesses of the western way of life. We see them in the efforts to construct a better alternative that are going on in what we may loosely term socialist as well as in many Christian experiments in community.

Indeed, the three vows of the more traditional forms of the Christian common life are particularly apt today in that they can, if lived out in a meaningful way, teach the western world a much-needed lesson. They can show it, in fact, that the evils of *enforced* chastity, poverty and obedience will never be eradicated unless it takes on some form of *voluntary* chastity, poverty and obedience after the example of this particular religious group. The vows of religion, in other words, exist for the sake of community. Their purpose is to foster and promote human fellowship within the individual Christian community, the community of the universal Church, and the community of all mankind.

Voluntary chastity is vital to the west today. Human beings must learn, after all, to transcend the limitations to their love that would confine it within the ties of sex or blood. They must be encouraged to extend their generosity beyond the limits of the family circle, the tribe or clan, the nation and their own ethnic group if the whole human race is ever to live as one family, according to God's purposes made plain in Jesus Christ and to the desires of the best of men.

Families and nations must learn, that is to say, to break out of the confines of their own self-interest and seek to welcome the stranger, black or white, and to bring in the lonely to the warmth of their love. They must show their readiness to forgo something of the comfort that they looked to from a steeply-rising standard of living in favour of the poor. And they must seek out ways, without violation of conscience, of curtailing that fullest expression of the love between husband and wife that is the begetting of children in order to show their wider love for the future generations whose very existence is threatened by over-population.

The religious community, if its celibate life is to be of value as a form of Christian witness that speaks to the men and women of our own day and age, ought to be a powerful reminder of this need in the west for a form of chastity freely undertaken. For here is a group of human beings drawn together not by sexual attraction, family relationship or common origin but by an affectionate, personal and self-sacrificing love such as can normally be found only in the bounds of a loving family. And this is a love that does not restrict itself to the group, but one that urges it to open itself out generously towards the wider communities in which it is set. In other words, it is possible to go beyond the joys of sexual love and family life and to forget national or racial pride and self-interest in order to live in brotherly and sisterly fashion with all, and particularly with those most in need of love.

Hence the demand, in religious associations of this kind, first, that they should become real communities and not just cold and heartless institutions, which means that they must be of such a size that the members can really learn, in brotherly or sisterly fashion, to *care* for one another; and, second, that they open their doors to the stranger, the misfit, the homeless, the lonely – not as an act of bounty but as a duty owed to needy members of the one human family. Thus the truly chaste community should be the first in the locality to witness against racism, class prejudice, religious intolerance, sexual inequality and the oppression of the weak. It seems clear that, ideally, such a community should be composed not merely of members from one nation, class or sex, and not simply, in a multi-racial society, of whites or blacks if it is to be a credible image of the future community of all mankind for which the west should be working and to which the Christian Church is dedicated.

But voluntary chastity goes further than this. It demands that the celibate community concern itself, too, with those threats to family living that we have already spoken of. It should be ready, somehow, to relieve the tensions of the nuclear family – even if only by helping individual families in their difficulties or by doing a spot of baby-sitting so that young couples can together escape the confines of the home for a time. But it must also be ready to protest not merely against what it may consider to be particularly pressing ethical problems like abortion and divorce but even more so against their causes. It must proclaim by its way of living that genuine harmony and affection is possible within any group of human beings, given the spirit of generosity and self-sacrifice. And it must go further and make known its objection to the very conditions that often restrict a family's love unjustly from without – against rampant commercialism, poor housing, low wages or forcible separations of parents from children or husband from family that are often imposed by local authorities or working conditions.

Voluntary poverty, or a change of heart by the rich, is an inescapable requirement if we are ever to arrive at one world in which all human beings can find enough to eat and the wherewithal to live as they deserve. In other words, the wealthy nations and institutions of the west must be prepared freely to give up their pursuit of profit whenever it exploits the poor, and must rather seek to give away something of their riches as a matter of justice to meet the needs of their fellow human beings.

And they ought to be encouraged to do so by the sign of poverty they see in the religious communities. Not only should these live as the poorer sections of the society in which they are situated, therefore, but they should also show themselves to be devoted in a special way to the service of the poor. Religious poverty does not mean merely a simplicity of house or dress or menu. It means taking on the insecurity and responsibility felt by the lowly and the humble who must work for their bread day by day and find the rent to pay for accommodation they will never own.

The work undertaken by the family-sized groups of dedicated Christians ought to be marked, too, by its quality of service to the poor. And this service may be of two kinds. It may be the taking up of some kind of welfare work or community service that directly helps the poor, at home or abroad. Or it may take the form of identifying more strictly with the poor by sharing their working conditions and labouring alongside them on the factory floor, at the workbench or on the assembly-line.

Indeed, the poor community will try to show, by its own way of living, that genuine personal fulfillment is only possible when one abandons the selfish exploitation of men and matter and treats of the world as made for man, and work as the joyful mastering of the material universe for its own development and the good of the whole human family. Poverty requires, in other words, that Christians take up a brotherly and sisterly attitude not only to their fellow human beings but also to the world itself. For the risen Christ not only displays to all men and women that they are in fact brothers and sisters in him their elder brother, and that their union will ultimately find completion when they share his state in glory, but also that matter itself is involved in this destiny, since it is man's partner on his journey towards the kingdom, and in brotherly fashion offers itself to him to be used by him to help draw the whole race more closely together in love.

A simple way of life, identification with the poor and a loving respect for the environment – all these are demanded if the Christian community is to witness to the need for voluntary poverty on the part of the rich. But it cannot stop there.

We are told that the slums of New York are crowded with communities of this type, all fervently dedicated to the kind of poverty we have been dealing with. And they are coming to realise that their witness can do no more than scratch the surface of a problem that can only be solved satisfactorily by political action.

In other words, the vow of poverty demands that communities protest by political commitment and activity as well as by their own life-style against the dehumanising conditions of the kind of work often imposed upon human beings by the needs of the modern industrial system and the production lines that cease not day nor night; against the steady destruction of our earth and air and water that this at present involves; and against the way the rich nations conduct their business overseas at the expense of the millions of poor and hungry people of the Third World.

It is the greatest tragedy, consequently, when religious communities seem instead little interested in the outside world but bent, rather, upon maintaining themselves and their institutions in the style to which they have become accustomed, and that at almost any cost. Nuns, for example, can be as ruthlessly exploited and overworked by their communities as the defenceless poor, and not for the sake of any kind of Christian witness, but merely to keep open a cherished school or nursing-home when these are no longer serving any real need save that of providing a regular income for a dwindling group of sisters.

An enforced and inhuman kind of poverty can be found, too, in communities where the vow is interpreted too legalistically and negatively, and where it is not, in fact, geared towards a better community life in which the brothers and sisters freely share all that they have, including their time and their concern, with one another and with the needy around them. For, if the community is too large to allow for this sharing process, and if the individual religious is deprived of all possession in the mistaken assumption that, however grand the community building and its appointments might be, this personal destitution is true religious poverty, then the result will be disruptive of all community.

Religious, instead of being open to their brethren, will instead become defensive, staking their claim to what little territory they may call their own and clinging on to it as tenaciously as any other mammal will do in overcrowded conditions. Their world will thus shrink to the size of their own room and their own heart, and the outside community will be seen as a threat to this little space that alone makes them feel they belong to the planet earth. Poverty does not, therefore, mean creating deprived persons within convent or monastery, but helping Christians to live in more sisterly and brotherly fashion within the family of man.

Voluntary obedience on the part of the powerful is another requirement if we are ever to arrive at peace on earth and good will among men. If human beings are to find true fellowship in love and peace, it will only be when the rulers of nations and the personal forces that shape our lives have learned to obey the needs of the human community. In other words, they must come to see their authority not in terms of enforced obedience but as a service meant to help all the peoples of this world – and not just the ruling classes or nations – to the enjoyment of a better and more fully human way of life.

Obedience to the human community, or the endeavour to help mankind to live in loving harmony, is not put into practice by the mere issuing of paternalistic directives from above but through consultation with and participation by all concerned – the citizens of town or state, the workers in the factory, and the hordes of the dispossessed whose voices must be heard in the councils of the great.

This pattern of obedience should therefore be exemplified in the way a Christian community is run and organised. The former Jesuitical empasis on a military-style discipline which divided a community up effectually into superior and subjects is out of touch with present-day needs and social patterns. Its witness would seem rather to support dictatorships than to draw the attention of secular authority to its responsibility towards the need of the human community for deeper fellowship. This is the law of love that all human beings must learn to obey if the race is to survive.

As Gabriel Moran and Maria Harris have said in their book *Experiences in Community* (Burns and Oates, 1969), 'A community by definition excludes a superior. . . . A com-union is a sharing of life, a joining in partnership, a giving in reciprocity and a union of equals. It is conceivable that one could be superior *to* a community, but it is impossible to be a superior *in* a community.' In other words, whoever may possess a leadership or administrative or directive or inspirational role within the community, it is still the community as such that alone can discover how better to obey the law of love and discern what its demands may be in the present circumstances.

That is why we may say that the basic rule of this kind of Christian living as of any other is the law of the gospel. For the model to which the community tries to conform itself is the life of Jesus, the man for others, and the love it seeks to live by is his risen life, the Holy Spirit. It is to the Spirit of Christ, then, that the community makes its vow of obedience – a Spirit that is present and at work not simply in leader or chairman but in the whole group. But the Spirit will only be heard in a human way by means of dialogue, consultation and the participation of all in the decision-making process.

In this way the Christian community can make telling witness to the reality of authority as a gift of God. For it thus makes plain its belief that it is the Spirit of Christ that men are in fact obeying when they try to bring about a greater human fellowship in the world. This Spirit, present in the community of man and voicing its demands whenever one human being asks another for his help, is the true law of Christians as of all mankind, and must become the guide of the powerful and the great if peace on earth is ever to be achieved.

This witness is vitiated wherever human rights are denied. And it is weakened where the struggle for human rights is shirked. This means that the Christian community must make sure that it plays no part itself in suppressing the rights of others, and that it is prepared to take up suitable political means to win justice for the oppressed.

For basic human rights can be denied within religious communities where the vow of obedience is interpreted in an authoritarian and dictatorial fashion.

For example, a brother or sister can be denied by the authorities in the community the basic human right to the kind of education to which he or she is most fitted, as though, in the west, this were still some kind of privilege to be handed out at the whim of a patron. Or the right to personal privacy can be invaded when the letters of members of the community are opened and read without their permission. The human right to work, and to that kind of work best suited to the individual's talents, is denied when the community member is simply drafted into whatever occupation the authorities think fit, without prior consultation. And the need for companionship and community life, without which there can be no real personal development as a human being, is also denied when certain members of the community are made into superiors in the sense condemned by Gabriel Moran, and thereupon cease from belonging to the community.

Thus voluntary chastity, poverty and obedience on the part of Christian communities are meant to make plain the need, in the west, for some kind of chastity, poverty and obedience to be freely undertaken by all if the unity of mankind is ever to come about. Furthermore, the communities also proclaim that such an endeavour is to share in the chaste, poor and obedient love of Jesus, and to allow room in our world for his Spirit to weld the race more firmly together until the kingdom of everlasting peace shall finally come, as come it must. And so the Christian community lives and witnesses in the way that it does, not as an exercise in self-discipline or self-restraint, but *for the sake of the kingdom of heaven*.

But there are further questions that are being widely asked today.

Are lifelong vows, for instance, an essential ingredient of this kind of witness? The idea of the permanent vow was very acceptable in feudal times or in a more static and stratified society, when one's occupation and station were chosen or imposed for life. But such a vow has no warranty in scripture, so that we may well ask whether the notion is applicable in the present day, when people are far more flexible in the work they do and in the way they choose to live.

It may be objected that, after all, marriage is still meant ideally to be a stable and permanent way of life. Why not, therefore, that of the monk or nun? But this is to forget that the human animal naturally forms a permanent bond with its mate, the breaking of which is always regrettable and distressing. A form of community life that does without marriage and family is, however, much more fragile and precarious since unnatural and therefore instinctually difficult. And some people may find they cannot permanently live this way.

So it is being asked whether permanent vows might not be scrapped in favour of a daily commitment or pledge or promise to this particular form of the Christian life. For some, this might result in a lifelong dedication. For others, perhaps only a year or two would be devoted to this particular way of witnessing to the gospel. Yet, in either case, many feel that the commitment would tend to be much more genuine and conscious, since those no longer committed would simply leave for some other kind of Christian living in no way inferior or less demanding of itself.

And then, need the voluntary chastity, poverty and obedience of the community be of the same kind in every case and for every member? Could not the group also include couples who wished to witness through marriage to the chastity to which the community is dedicated? Could not the extent to which members wished to share their lives or possessions be left more to the individual, according to the degree of involvement with which he or she is able to cope?

These are the kinds of question being asked in those Christian communities that are alive to the spirit and needs of the day and that are in consequence more attractive to the young. As we see all around us, those other communities that are still hidebound by spurious traditions or tied down to outdated customs are in fact rapidly dying out. And the sooner the better, since in this case they are patently failing to witness to the gospel ideal of community life in a manner relevant to the western world of the 1970s.

I should like to end this chapter and this book with what to me seems a striking and prophetic example of the way some Christians are striving to reshape in non-escapist and non-magical terms the notion of the alternative society. Here, then, is a present-day equivalent of the ancient 'Holy Rules' of the great alternative societies of the past, the religious orders. It is entitled *The Search for a Liberating Life-style*, and is the manifesto, as it were, of an ecumenical community centred in *Emmaus House*, East Harlem, and led by David Kirk, a priest of the melchite rite in communion with the Roman Catholic Church.

'We have no guidelines, but a few clues so far: SEEKING itself is part of the style, we are fellow-travellers on the road, in human solidarity with every man who seeks a fully human life.

'IN JESUS CHRIST, the first of the New Men, a new way of living is revealed. The resurrection of wholeness begins. The Way is not outside us: nor is it hidden: nor is it the prize at the end. It is within us: we are there, the kingdom is *now*.

' "THE WAY IS NEAR but men seek it afar. It is in easy things but men seek it in difficult things." A Zen saying.

'THE PRIMACY OF LOVE, which leads to sharing, to listening, to dying, to giving one's life for one's friends.

'FAITH which transcends sectarianism and pettiness, and HOPE which allows a future for everybody's potential.

'THE NEW ASCETICISM: CREATIVITY. Instead of dead formulas, "obedience", "humility", "renunciation", instead of renouncing or even overcoming the world, we propose to *transform* it, to dare to create a new thing. If the Holy Spirit is the revelation of creativity, we must not blaspheme the Spirit with our deadness and immovability.

'YOUTHFULNESS (spiritually) with nothing to lose by change, nothing invested. The carefree life of the Gospel!

'PLAYFULNESS which keeps us from taking ourselves too seriously, opens up work as "play with problems" and liturgy as "leisure time" and relieves intensive community. Indeed, reality is not always intelligible: truth often comes to Emmaus in the guise of Harpo Marx!

'A NEW SENSE OF TIME: less a servant of automatic time, one lives by the meaning one chooses, and in the *present*.

'A CAPACITY FOR WONDER: man as child, environment as toy.

'EXPERIENCE OF BECOMING A PERSON, of having autonomy: being a person, not a thing: of finding power to affirm values.

'INTENSIVE COMMUNITY: we are urban nomads in a mobile, temporary society, where informality, lack of traditional social props help people relate immediately, even intensely.

'THE PERSONAL AND THE COMMUNAL: a kind of partnership, with room for privacy and commonness, with "psychic densities" which match the physical densities of New York City.

'PERMANENTLY CHANGING: there are no new stabilities to replace the old ones: those who are alive identify with the adaptive process. We are dealing with change and its *consequences*.

'INSECURITY: which means vulnerability of property, money, memory, ego, etc.

'DE-CENTRALIST HUMANISING ORGANISATION: we are working out a decentralist experiment, with authority based on function as a communal responsibility.

'WE ARE LEARNING COMMUNALLY:

   'a concept of *power* based on co-operation and reason rather than coercion and hierarchical rules;

   'a concept of *man* based on transfiguration and an increasing understanding of the complexity of man;

   'a concept of *organisation* which actualises human potential.

'WE ARE ALL NIGGERS NOW: HUMAN SOLIDARITY: after the recent persecution of the Black Panthers we are all Niggers now. We express solidarity with all those who seek to build the new mankind:

   '(1) an end to the war in Vietnam;
   '(2) meaningful community control of schools;
   '(3) support of the Black Liberation Movement for a share in the power, property and wealth of the U.S.;
   '(4) support of the student movement to end the complicity of the university in war, imperialism and racism;
   '(5) confront the white problem by confronting whites with the destructive system;
   '(6) democratically restructuring social institutions;
   '(7) support the redistribution of wealth, property and power everywhere;

'(8) support a guaranteed income and freedom budget to end poverty.

'WE ARE ON THE FRONTIERS OF REVOLUTION: with many questions and few answers. We live in tension with most movements to the extent that we try to be agents of reconciliation.'